Lessons from Behind the Counter

The Principles a Business Family Uses to Empower Future Generations

Robin Estevez

Lessons from Behind the Counter

Printed by:
CreateSpace Independent
Publishing Platform

Copyright © 2017, Robin Estevez

Published in the United States of America

140310-001

ISBN-13: 978-1544687483
ISBN-10: 1544687486

For more information on 90-Minute Books including finding out how you can
publish your own lead generating book, visit www.90minutebooks.com or call
(863) 318-0464

Here's What's Inside…

For Ingrid, who always believes in me.

"I truly believe we can either see the connections, celebrate them, and express gratitude for our blessings, or we can see life as a string of coincidences that have no meaning or connection. For me, I'm going to believe in miracles, celebrate life, rejoice in the views of eternity, and hope my choices will create a positive ripple effect in the lives of others. This is my choice." -*Mike Ericksen*

Prologue

From the time I was a child, I've had a profound respect for those who are able to create something from nothing. The type of people who can move *pa'lante* - onward no matter what may be blocking their way while never failing to uplift those around them. They only see opportunities where others see an obstacle.

My father Morel and my uncle Pachango are these type of people. Two brothers whose love and respect for each other is unmatched. It's the kind of relationship I want to emulate with my brothers and sister. Through sheer will and desire, they raised their families while working alongside them, creating a business that continues to grow today. With a business that has evolved from a family business operating a single mom and pop bodega to a business family with multiple locations and interests.

This book is as much a way for me to honor both my father and uncle as it is to capture the lessons I've learned from working beside them. It's about how *cibaeños* (country folks) ingrained their same work ethic into their family. Immersing them in the culture and identity of their Dominican hometown, Corozo, while embracing an American life.

I would also like this book to serve as a guiding tool for my children, nieces, nephews, and the generations to come. Let it be an instrument they can use to create a greater future for themselves and their own families.

As Dad always said and continues to tell us, "It is your choice to live a good, healthy life."

To live well within your means and create a better future for your family, your team, community, and yourself. But you must want to live a good life — strong in faith, dedication and focus and one with the willingness to do the necessary work to live into it. Spending quality time with family and being open to bettering your community all make for a good, healthy life. However, living a good, healthy life may mean different things to each of us and it is up to us to make the right choices throughout our lives.

This is what makes up our core business mission today: To serve our neighbors and team by helping them lead a healthy life.

Within the pages of this book, you will learn the principles that enabled an immigrant family from the Dominican Republic to thrive in New York City. How they used their competitive advantage to live into the American Dream and help countless others reach their own success both in America and in their hometown of Corozo. These lessons will empower you to see through the obstacles and grasp onto opportunities allowing you to build a better future

.

Part One:
Lessons From Behind the Counter

A Can Full of Dreams

I'm son of the sweat earned in the

The back room de una bodega

Behind the counter

Reaching higher

Trying to place a can full of dreams on

The top shelf

I carry within me the sorrow

Of a husband

That only knows how to tend to his family

Tending to his risk

Assured only

By the warm plate served to his kids

Where he went with want

They know none

The only support he hears

Is the voice of his wife coming through

The phone stuck between his shoulder and ear

Asking for the 5th time,

"Love when are you coming home?"

1
From the Aisles

"Where did you grow up?"

I get asked this question often.

If I had to pick one place, I'd have to say I grew up in my father's supermarket. Within the aisles, between and behind the displays; pushing a broom, at the cash register, making deliveries is where I grew up. I watched all of our different neighbors come in shopping, say "hello," and pat me on the head. I grew up working alongside my brothers and sister, my father, aunts and uncles, and many others who became an extension of my family. I learned through them and saw myself in each of them.

So, where did I grow up?

Yes, I went to bed, woke up, and went to school in Hackensack, New Jersey. Yet, so much of my life was crossing over the George Washington Bridge on a bus to work alongside my family at our business in the Bronx - Parkchester neighborhood.

Being a kid, I didn't want to work all the time, but I had to work. You see, in our household, we had a core belief that was a part of everything we did: *Through hard work and a strong desire to succeed, then anything can and will be overcome.*

We were (and still are) your typical American family working to achieve the American Dream. We see America as one of the only places in the world where you could have a dream and actually obtain it. We're from the Dominican Republic; the land of baseball, white sand beaches, and merengue. My parents are Maria and Juan Estevez—Mami and Papi. Mami, pregnant with my older brother, came to New York in 1968. Papi followed and arrived about a year later. My siblings and I were born in New York City. There's four of us: John, Maggie, Billy, and me.

Even though there are only six of us in our immediate family, we've always had extended family members living with us. I once counted fifteen people living under the Estevez roof at our house in Hackensack. In addition to the six of us, there were several aunts, uncles, and cousins living with us along with one of my grandfathers. Most of my extended family came with us when we moved from Washington Heights, the Dominican enclave, where most residents from the island move to once they arrived to the United States.

I can still remember the grown-ups in the small kitchen eating area. Some were sitting and some were standing while the kids sat on the stairs. I recall my Aunt Anny doing her hair in the upstairs bathroom with the door open and all of us listening to my father talk about what happened at one of the two stores. Magdaline Grocery, his bodega named after my sister, and the new C-Town Supermarket he just bought. He would fill us in on the everything that happen; teaching, worrying, pushing, planting, sowing, striving, succeeding.

Anyone who knows and loves my father calls him Morel. It's a nickname he got as a baby from an uncle who would put him to sleep singing "Juanita Morel" by Tatico Herinquez. It was always funny when a new vendor came into the store and would walk right up to my father and ask for him by his first name Juan. A lot of times my father would string him along to find out if the vendor was worth talking to, to get a better price, or to gain some other insight. Still today, if you walked into any of our stores and happen to bump into Papi, you would never think he was the owner. Papi can and *will* outwork and hustle us all.

At work, we never called him Papi—it was always Morel. Although it may sound kind of weird for us as kids calling him Morel instead Papi, it served a purpose. I think it was one of his ways of letting us know although we were his children, we were not going to be coddled at work. So, in the stores it was always Morel and at home and everywhere else, it was Papi.

Morel has taught me how to become and behave as a man. He led my brothers, sister, and I to fully understand what it takes to build a business from the ground up. We lived and breathed the business so that we knew how to make it prosper. While raising his own, he supported countless families by successfully running the stores. Papi taught me how to be a devoted husband and loving father. I'm not sure about my siblings, but he became my hero — he still is, and will always be. He believed and nurtured our capabilities while cultivating the men and woman we would become. Papi ingrained in us to believe and work towards the power of a unified family— the strength of which could not be matched. So as long as the Estevez family remained one unit, we would overcome and succeed. Understanding that building a unified family takes effort, Papi gave us the skills to raise our own family even though he never had a father of his own to teach him how to raise his.

My experiences aren't unique to me. My brothers and cousins all had similar experiences. There were countless other Dominican families doing the same thing that we were. They worked "iron hours"—from the time the iron gates went up until they came down. Though most of us were born and raised in the New York area, our upbringing was old school Dominican Republic. Our community is still very much about the family unit, hard work, faith, and getting ahead. We were raised with the hunger to succeed and saw firsthand what failure looked like. A true immigrant mindset was burnished into our psyches— one in which nothing should be taken for granted. Really there was only one objective, and it was to succeed. The only way to succeed was by consistently working hard, gathering the tools and/or resources you could, most of which came through extended family networks.

Life Lesson

Getting to work alongside your family will teach you about struggle, sacrifice, and the success of building a business from the ground up in order to obtain the American Dream.

2
Fired Up and Fired Down

My father taught me not only to always show respect, but also to have a healthy disdain towards arrogance. This respect was all-encompassing; respect for family and for yourself, respect for our neighbors who would spend their hard-earned money with us, respect for our team whom we would work with everyday side-by-side, and most importantly, respect for the business that supported us all.

You see, in our family, respect for the business was and remains paramount. If you treat the business with respect, it will reward you with a profit. A healthy friendship requires you to spend time with the other person. You make memories, nurture, and give-and-take. You reach out to each other and strive together. Without those things, the friendship begins to fade. Without enough contact, the distance becomes too great to maintain the strong ties. You should treat a business with the same respect offered to a friend by spending time in it and cultivating it. You take time to see and get to know all its little nuances. You learn that just like the friend who supported you during a rough patch, the business too will push you forward and sustain you. It will push you ahead to bigger possibilities. However, this can only happen from the amount of respect you show it.

Papi would point out to us other seemingly successful businessmen or politicians who looked like they had everything in the world, including the respect that went with their outward success. Then he would show us how they treated their staff, their children, or the vendors. We would see that their behavior was inconsistent. He would reveal to us that the respect those few thought they had, was just an illusion. They couldn't be respected because their actions were not in line with who they truly were which was arrogant. A trait that is despised by most.

I remember being raked over the coals by my dad when I was a kid for beginning to think and act like I was the privileged boss's son. Somehow, when I was 14 years old, I'd gotten it into my head that I was "the boss," because I helped to hire and let folks go. I was responsible for managing the store front, opening and closing, and making sure everyone was doing their jobs. I would count out the registers and go to the bank. I even got friendly with the cashiers and hung out with the stock boys. I would come in late and then left when I wanted. I mean, I was a big boss, so I really could do as I pleased … or so I thought.

Zig Ziglar once said "Conceit is a weird disease. It makes everybody sick except the one who's got it." And everyone was basically fed up with me.

On one particular day my bratty self was in full-bloom. On this day my sister was working the office and I was tending to the front. Really though, I was fooling around as only 14-year-old boys know how to do around a bunch of girls. Only these weren't just any girls—they were the cashiers in a business and much older than me.

The office sits about 12 feet above and 15 feet away from the registers, so you can get a full view of the store from there. Maggie was in the office witnessing all of my antics and taking into account each and every one of them. I was below, yelling orders up to her. She was not having it and in turn responded over the PA system back to me. Poor Maggie, I'd just roped her in with me. Just like brothers and sisters do, we got louder and louder. She began arguing for me to just do my job and stop messing around. At some point, I stormed into the office and started cursing at Maggie. We went back and forth without realizing that the mic was on. We dropped more than a few F-bombs at each other over the PA system.

Racing up the stairs in full sprint, Dad ran in and yanked the mic off the wall. He threw it to the floor in disgust. We froze. Neither of us said a word, believing that if we didn't move or make a sound, then Dad wouldn't notice us. As Dad turned around, it seemed like an eternity, we both got the biggest verbal ass-whipping of our lives. He fired us both, right then and there. With tears in our eyes, he told us to leave right in the middle of the day. To get on the bus and go home.

We protested our firing. "But we're your kids! Who's going to open tomorrow? Who will close?"

"You're not needed, it's none of your concern."

We had been fired, just like any other employee not doing his or her job.

Later at home, after the longest bus ride from the Bronx to New Jersey, the fear set in. Maggie and I knew that we messed up, but being fired was impossible. That was our father. Later that night, we figured he would talk to us, we would repent with tears in our eyes, and then we would be working tomorrow as usual.

We didn't see him that night, so the next morning we were up and ready to go early. As usual, we waited in the kitchen as Dad grabbed his coffee and headed to the door. Then we got up to leave.

He stopped us in our tracks saying, "*Y para donde ustedes crean que van?*"

Where do you two think you are going?

That's when it hit us—we weren't needed. We wouldn't be asked to help.

For three months we languished at home, not helping and watching everyone else leave. Later we would have to hear the stories and the day's happenings. We were out of the loop.

Looking back, the greatest lesson I learned was a lesson about humility. My own arrogance had blinded me from seeing the true reasons why both Maggie and I were there. Simply put, we were there to serve our neighbors and community, to work alongside our father, and to help build the business. We were supposed to be united; to act and be one. We were there to contribute and be a part of something greater than us. We were there to learn and uplift the family.

But I hadn't seen that immediately. All I felt at first was the pain of not being able to go to work. The store was truly the one place where any of us was able to really spend time with our father--whether we were behind the counter at la bodega grinding coffee, at a register in the supermarket, riding with him from La Marketa to stock up on the day's supplies, learning to build a display, or making a sign.

For me, I see it as a privilege to be able to work alongside my father, brothers, sister, and our extended family which includes everyone on our team. I will forever respect the privilege and honor with all whom I get to work with shoulder-to-shoulder, growing, learning, struggling and succeeding while always having a bit of fun.

Life Lesson

You cannot allow arrogance to cloud the privilege to contribute to something greater than yourself. The respect you desire must be earned. You must first recognize it and give it to others before you ever have it.

3
A Heavy Key Chain

As soon as John was old enough to drive, Dad sent us to open the store on our own. He would take the time to sleep in "late" and arrive with Maggie at the supermarket around 9:00 a.m. In the meantime, John and I had to make sure to open up on time, no matter the weather. We learned how to time the traffic on the George Washington Bridge while taking into account the time needed if we had to pick anyone up along the way. If you were the one getting picked up for a ride to the store and weren't at the designated spot on time, we left you—just like Dad would've. Just like he had left us countless times for not being punctual. The store needed to be open for business by 7:00 a.m. This meant we needed to arrive at least 15 minutes ahead of opening time.

Essentially, we were two kids, John at 17 and me at 11, with a heavy ring of keys dangling by a loop on our jeans. It seemed like there were over 100 keys dangling from the loop, all heavier than me. I knew each key by order on the ring and its feel. Lock by lock, we would open and roll up the gates. The butchers, produce clerks, stock guys, and cashiers were all older than us. They stood and watched us push those heavy iron gates up in the heavy heat, dripping rain, or dead cold. In winter sometimes the locks would freeze overnight and we would have to ask one of the butchers or stock clerks for part of their beloved Sports section. By rolling up the newspaper and lighting it with a match we were able to create a crude version of a torch that we then put directly to the locks to warm them and open the gates up. *Clack, clack, clack—Boom!* — they would go as we pushed them up. It was a sound so distinct—the *clack, clack, clack* of the iron gates -- the gates that kept the thieves out while at the same time kept us in working iron hours.

John and I were—opening up, assigning tasks, checking and paying out vendors, watching over it all. If someone failed to show, we would fill in. I learned a lot during those years riding in the car with John, picking up uncles and others in the crew. I heard some things that for a young boy at 11, would've made my mother blush.

We always had responsibility. On a Saturday morning while most kids were sleeping, John and I were throwing open the gates. When other kids were waking up later and still in their PJs watching Saturday morning cartoons with a bowl of cereal, we were unloading trucks and looking out for shoplifters. By the time the afternoon Kung Fu movies came on, John and I had set stock, made a few displays, tended to the front, counted out registers, and swept the store. We learned to do it all alongside our father.

Sometimes I ask myself why my father trusted two kids with the keys to the store. It was a question he answered many years later.

As it turns out, Dad told me this:

"I wanted you, your brothers and sister to know the struggles, success, and effort it takes to create something. To have respect for the work we were doing building a business. Together as a family. It was a risk I took with you at a young age during the rough New York City times. But I believed in you. I would take Maggie and John with me to La Marketa to get all the supplies, waking them up before dawn so they saw and felt what it took to make it. You always came to the bodega. All I wanted was to grow with you and build something for my family with my family."

Life Lesson

When you're given trust to prove worthy of a responsibility, make sure to uphold your part because the amount of trust earned is in direct correlation to the effort you give.

4
Joke's On Me

On very long days, we would take turns napping in the store's basement on top of boxes. I would line up boxes filled with paper towels or bathroom tissue and this would become my bed for the next hour or so. A 20-pound sack of rice would be my pillow. If I got cold, I would grab a few of the butchers' white coats to use as a blanket. My resting place would be between stacks of beans and other canned goods piled high on each side. Most men would have to sidestep in order to walk down the tight corridor filled with coffee, rice, and soda stacked from floor to ceiling. Most of the time, I would be sure to close off the foot of my makeshift bed with more boxes, so anyone passing by would never know I was there. Plus, it added the benefit of dampening the noise in the busy basement storage area where there was constant movement.

During school breaks and summer vacations, wake-up call would be around 4:00 a.m., which had us at the store by 5:00 a.m. to unload trucks. It was a crazy crew: Me, Dad, John, and the stock guys whom we made sure to pick up along the way since the buses didn't run that early in the morning. Otherwise we would have been stuck unloading on our own. Piece by piece, the truck got unloaded. We'd have to make sure the count was right, sorted, and pushed out to the aisles. By opening time at 7:00 a.m., Dad bought everyone breakfast and announced a bounty prize of an extra fifty dollars on the spot to the guy who stocked the most cases. A ton of product would've been already put onto the shelves before the first customer arrived—but Dad wanted to be sure that every last box was out of the way, so he would make the incentive to get a last push from the guys.

On days like this, I would be breaking down cardboard boxes, moving from aisle to aisle helping the guys or grabbing a wayward box of peanut butter that had somehow ended up in the soap aisle. Back then, everything had to be priced-marked with label guns. I can remember Luis in aisle two with a label gun in each hand, pricing two boxes of items at the same time. No one else could ever do it and I was shocked the first time I saw it.

The guys all had funny nicknames like El Principe, Ketchup, and El Zorro. Each was more funny and weirder than the other. In those times, Dad seemed to always get some guys who might have resorted to other things had they not been given a job by my father. I couldn't believe the chances Dad took with some of them. Later he would explain to John and I that some of those kids had never been taught to work. All they needed was to keep themselves busy, learn, stay out of trouble, and they could make it.

I've experienced everything and just about anything within the supermarket environment. From the exhilaration of opening a new store with so many people wanting to shop with us that firefighters were doing crowd-control to maintain capacity, to my first crush and the heartbreak of rejection even to kissing an older girl and learning about deceit by a trusted confidant.

But the one thing I will never forget would be my greatest embarrassment…

I was spending my weeks of summer vacation in the aisles, but itching to be outside in the summer sun. The floor crew at the time was made up of older guys ranging from 17 to 23 years old. I saw them as cool, impressive dudes. I loved the stories they told of racing cars, getting girls, and partying it up. I was trying be just as cool as they were. Only I wasn't. I was just a punk little kid, trying to fit in. So I started playing pranks on them; disordering their aisles, hiding their label guns, mixing up the cases from aisle to aisle—just making their jobs harder. It got to the point where some got into trouble with Dad for not getting their jobs done on time. And so they began to plot their revenge on me.

Every day at lunchtime, everyone would chip in cash and someone would run out to pick up food. Then the person would set it up buffet-style for all to share. On this day, all seemed normal to me. I put in my three dollars and was called down to eat when the food arrived. The crew was already gathering around the table. As I went to sit, a hood was placed over my head from behind me, so I couldn't see. Then they began to strip me naked. I could still hear the laughter and their yelling to me, "You like to play pranks? This is payback!"

But that's not the worst of it. In the distance we could hear my father's keys jingling as they hung from his pants loop. He was coming down the stairs talking to someone. A signal was given. All the guys scattered and hid among the boxes. With my naked self still on the floor, I stood up and pulled the hood off my head just as dad and a saleswoman turned the corner. There I stood in all my 13-year-old glory—completely naked with only socks on my feet.

Dad and the saleswoman stood frozen, speechless at the sight of me. I glanced around but didn't see my clothes so I ran to hide in the farthest corner of the basement by the refrigeration motors. I heard the keys as they were walking away. When I thought it was safe, I sneaked around the deserted basement looking for my clothes. They were still nowhere to be found.

The only one not involved was my brother John. It was probably because he was busy doing a delivery. From what I later heard, the guys miraculously were all in the aisles working, having escaped by a second set of stairs in another part of the basement, when Dad reappeared upstairs in the store. He apologized to the saleswoman and made an appointment for another day.

While steam still rose from the untouched food, no one ate lunch that day. All the guys acted shocked to hear what had happened. When John finally came back from his deliveries, Dad told him what happened. For four hours, I stood naked in the basement, locked up in one of the bathrooms. As if I had the plague, no one came near me for fear of catching the riot act from my father.

Finally, John not being able to find my clothes except for my sneakers, went out and bought me underwear, sweats, and a hoodie. He then scooted me out of the store and took me home. The guys had gotten their payback for all the pranks I'd played on them. That was the story and the truth. I took full blame for the "naked kid in the basement incident." No one got into trouble. They all had feared getting fired, but I refused to say who was involved.

Nothing more needed to be said. I'd learned my lesson and now had been fired for a second time.

A few weeks later, Mami and I caught a ride to the store with one of the guys working in the store at that time. As we were approaching the bridge crossing into New York City, Mami asked me again for the millionth time, "Robin, what was it that happened to you that day in the supermarket?" Knowing exactly what happened to me that day, he tensed up and put the grip of death on the steering wheel while waiting for my answer.

Without missing a beat, I repeated back, "Mom, just some of the guys fooling around with me."

That sealed it. I was one of the boys.

Life Lesson

There is no "I" in "team." Only when you respect the efforts of those around you, help them achieve their goals, and are willing to strive along with them will you become part of the team.

5
Up for Interpretation

Dad couldn't speak English too well, just enough to get by. Whenever he had an important meeting with a lender, at the warehouse or an attorney, he would pull John and I out of school or keep us home. We attended a lot of meetings as kids. He taught us to listen and focus on how things were said, who said what, their mannerisms, the tone, and context. Teaching us listening was more important than talking.

John, as the eldest, was the main interpreter and I was the backup. Many people would not know who I was or just thought I was a kid not paying attention, so they would speak freely or review in front of me. All the while not knowing I was keeping mental notes to fill in Dad of what was being said when he was not present-- whether it be in the bathroom or in waiting room.

John and I sat through so many different meetings with lawyers, bankers, vendors, waste collectors, government officials, auditors, accountants, and other business owners. Dad wanted us to know about all of it; to understand the business inside and out. From working the stores, to negotiating deals, we experienced the pain or delight that would come out of some of these conversations. We helped lighten the mood and soothe tensions. We heard our fair share of curse words in just about every language and became experts in both English and Spanish. We learned who liked to drink, gamble, and who had a mistress. We learned to see past the suits and ties, fancy desks, and plaques on the walls to truly see that the men sitting across from us were men just like us.

Some were willing to help us, and some, not so much. We learned that things weren't always as they seemed and that respect went a long way, especially when a favor was needed. We learned when to walk away or fight to the end. When we got bullied, we did the only thing a bully responds to—fighting back on our terms, diverting their energy, focusing on walking away unscathed, or punching them in the face. We learned to see how we were being seen. We learned to think under seemingly insurmountable pressure fast.

Really, we were just kids learning about ourselves, our father, the business, the people in it, and how the world worked. We learned that some of the biggest crooks would smile, give you a big bear hug, and fancy your every desire. The ones that helped you the most could be the most seemingly detestable and grotesque. We learned to pay dues both figuratively and literally. But probably one of the most important things we learned was not to take things at face value. Just like a dented can of corn that everyone discards and puts aside, 99.99% of the time, the kernels were just as delicious as if eaten from the cobb. They were perfectly fine and good enough to eat. We were to look at problems as opportunities offered to us and understanding they are a privilege for us to take on. Many others never even get the chance, didn't take it or didn't know what to do with those same opportunities.

There were the other times I had to baby-sit grown men in cheap suits. I couldn't stand to see them walking through the front door of the supermarket. Smelling of cigarettes, coffee, and cheap cologne. They were sometimes bleary eyed, never saying hello, never showing any respect. They walked in as if they owned the place. They would expect to just be let up to the office and tended to hand and foot but I would not. Dad would see or hear them from deep within the aisles where he was working, give me a nod if I was in sight to let them up to the office and send a message to John to deal with them. He avoided at all costs being directly involved with these guys who came every month. Some of the higher ups, yes, but not these guys. Inevitably I had to baby-sit, sometimes for hours in the office, bored to death, while they smoked the time away, drank black coffee and reading the *New York Daily News* trying to make conversation with me. Finally, John or dad would relieve me of my babysitting duties by sending me out on a delivery. I never knew what they said to make the cheap suits leave, but understood that their visits were just a part of the business that we were forced to live with.

At one point there was a change of guard and the new higher ups called us to a meeting at their headquarters. It was a beautiful place with wood panels and marble floors everywhere. From the sheer lavishness, you could tell it was the kind of place used to impress or intimidate. John and I were led into a big conference room and sat across from six grown men who had nothing better to do then try to bully us. Five were in cheap suits and one wore a custom-made suit. The guy in the custom made suit greets us by letting us know he didn't like our attitude and was huffing and puffing about respect and consequences. He was making what I thought was a big show of nothing. We honestly didn't care who or what he was or represented. As always, I had my notebook and pen and was jotting down notes and reference points. He saw what I was doing and blew up at me. I tell him it's my right to take notes or doodle to my heart's content. He comes around the table, stands behind me and lays his hands on my shoulders, squeezing into me, and explains in not the nicest way I needed to stop jotting down notes unless I was a lawyer. John taps my knee under the table and only then did I put away my pen and notebook. But thankfully, with God on our side, we were able to dodge a bullet and never saw them again.

Another time, for some reason, John wasn't able to go to a meeting with the wholesaler, our main grocery supplier. For weeks, there had been an ongoing argument between them and us, escalating every day as each delivery pulled up. I didn't understand much about it at the time but did not go to school that day because I had to fill in for John. Dad needed a translator, so it fell to me.

It was tense in the car as we pulled up to the wholesaler's offices. Dad had brought some papers and invoices from the store, his own pocket calculator that he still carries to this day. With me as his trusted interpreter, he had all the energy and vigor to fight an army.

What a sight! It was truly a David and Goliath moment.

We were escorted into a large, beautiful conference room with all the trimming and treats just an arm's length away by the receptionist.

As we waited to be seen, Dad patted me on the head and asked, "*Estas listo?*" - Are you ready?

In walks the head of the warehouse, completely old school. As soon as the pleasantries ended, it began. There was no letting up between them. Back and forth, Dad worked his calculator, using numbers from the invoices. He had caught the warehouse with their hand in the cookie jar—skimming an extra 3% to 5% on every load delivered—on top of charging a 24% interest rate on a loan.

"Where's your respect? Your loyalty? We helped you be where you are. Without us what would you have?" He said as he barreled down the far end of the conference table toward us.

Dad's face broke a sort of half smile before he responded.

"Your respect was lost as soon as you started stealing from me. You're just a thief dressed up in a tie. Helped me? I helped myself. I worked for everything I have. My family worked to pay off every single dollar—ahead of time. I owe you nothing. You owe me for what you have taken from me and my family. I have what I've made. You have taken more from me than what I ever owe you. Here I am busting my ass to make a nickel on a can of tuna. All the while, Mr. CEO is sitting on the beach drinking an ice cold beer with the wind cooling off his balls. Enjoying my hard earned money for himself."

Keep in mind I was 12 maybe, 13 years old at the time, and interpreting every curse word back and forth. Dad may not have been able to speak English too well, but he could understand most of it.

So here I was, a kid, cursing back at the old man sitting across from us because he was easier to face than Dad if I had not translated his every single word.

Life Lesson

Learn the language of others and what they are saying because listening is more than just hearing the words being said. Know when to keep quiet and when to speak up. Make sure to choose your words wisely because they can be used to tear down or uplift.

6
Connection to Tom and Jerry

Each night as I lay in bed at 7:00 p.m. watching the Cartoon Network with my six-year-old son, I'm transported to a different era. To a time when I was the same age that Matthew is now. This was a time when I was fragile, not knowing of the world, living in an apartment in Washington Heights on 175th Street between Audubon and St. Nicholas, across the street from the Incarnation Church. It is the apartment my parents chose to live in. One floor below my aunt and uncle, Lucila and Pachango, and their seven kids - my cousins Gabriel, Dennis, Manny, Maritza, Ramon, Millie, and Jose. It was our building; it was our place. In our 2-bedroom apartment, #44, up to eight or ten people, maybe a few more, lived there at some point. The number doesn't matter because we were all family. People were coming and going all the time. They were going to work in a factory or a bodega, La Marketa or picking up kids from school. It was a constant in-and-out flow of people. I remember my parents had a red velvet sofa with gold wood trim, covered in plastic so we wouldn't ruin it.

Thirty-six years later, I'm watching the same cartoons I used to watch on a small little TV at 3:00 p.m. every day. It was my favorite time of day because I was able to see my father. Every day he would leave at 4:30 a.m. to go to La Marketa to pick up the supplies, produce, meat, and everything else he needed for the day's sales. Each day he would wake up early and leave while all of us were in bed and he'd come back when all of us were tucked in again. The only time he had to see us during the day was between 3:00 p.m. to maybe 4:00 or 4:30 p.m. He would come home and eat a meal, freshen up and say to me "vamos a ver los muñequitos" - let's watch the cartoons - and I would tune the TV to the right channel.

We would lay on the plastic-covered sofa and in the summer, it would get so sticky that my mother would put down a towel so he wouldn't stick to it. He would lay there with me watching Tom and Jerry and inevitably would fall asleep. Me, as a typical five-year-old, would always shake and wake him saying "Papi, Papi, you're missing what Tom is doing to Jerry!" And he would look up, pat me on the head and say, "Si - yo estoy viendo" – Yes, I'm watching - keeping his eyes open for another second before falling back to sleep.

It was basically the only hour he had to rest during the day. Opening the bodega at 7:00 a.m., and closing it at midnight, there really was not much time for him to sleep. And soon enough, my mother would wake him. He would take another shower; drink a strong cup of black coffee and head out the door again for his second shift. Sometimes I would feel his kisses in the middle of the night. And I'm sure John and Maggie felt the same gentle kisses.

These were the sacrifices he made so that today, I am able to watch *Tom and Jerry* with my son, Matthew. It brings tears of respect to my eyes for all he was able to accomplish. Making my own sacrifices easier to bear.

Life Lesson

Recognize how far you've come. Appreciate the simple things and be grateful for the memories and moments you have today. Be grateful for the experiences you've lived and share them so they are not lost.

7
All Cracked Up

All day we'd been on the watch for the crazy dude to come back. Over and over again, a crazed guy wearing a fake fur bomber jacket in the New York City heat wave would make his way into our store with the intent to steal something to sell on the street for drugs. Over and over again, we would block his path, force him out, and grab back anything that he had taken.

Normally he would move from store to store, but on this particular day, he picked ours to constantly harass. We'd become his focus. This was a pattern repeating all over the city. These addicts would grab and steal something, sell or trade it on the street to buy more drugs and then do it all over again. As grocers, we had to employ people just to watch so that the shelves were not left bare. You ended up learning just by walking through the aisles if there had been a run on your store. Shelf by shelf, you could tell what products were potentially easy for theft. Because once word got out that your place was an easy mark, a swarm like locusts would make its way toward your store.

It was the early 1990s and New York was engulfed in the crack epidemic. There were addicts everywhere. You would see a nice college girl ride up from downtown Manhattan with her boyfriend, arm-in-arm, buy drugs, and then jump back on the train to head back to a "safer" part of town. When they were passing by the front of the store, I would recognize them because they were so out of place.

I would ask myself, "What are these kids with NYU and Columbia sweatshirts doing up here?"

The girl would eventually learn the route, so she did not need her boyfriend to make the trip uptown to Harlem anymore. We'd then see her latch onto the local big heavy guy, and we'd all just know what was going on. It played out every day on the street for all to see, not only in New York City but anywhere crack had its hold. Within weeks, sometimes days, the same girl that we'd seen jumping off the train holding her preppy boyfriend's hand and excited to be in a prohibited land, could be seen beat up or sleeping on a bench. Reeking, she looked like she aged five decades in a span of only two or three weeks. It was a terrible thing to witness. Unfortunately, we saw firsthand, all too often, innocence robbed by a glass pipe or needle.

Addicts would do just about anything for their next fix. The easiest target for them would be local shops where they could do a "grab and run." It was not uncommon to see two or three people chasing down a crackhead for a couple of steaks stolen from the store's case. This terrible disease just took over people's minds.

But, back to the fake fur wearing fiend. He just would not stop coming to our door, ramming through the aisles, knocking things and people over. Even some of the neighbors got involved and would block his approach. The local boys wouldn't sell to him because he was becoming more and more frantic to the point it was hurting their business by bringing too much unwanted attention. When the cops would arrive, they couldn't find him. Just as they pulled away, here he would come again. At one point, the assistant store manager pushed him out and ended up in a fistfight right on the curb. Shoppers just kept shopping because it was such a familiar sight around the neighborhood.

Finally, the fight broke off. He left and our manager went to clean up. Not ten minutes later, I was yelling for the keys because he was crossing the street and had a gun in his hand. Just as I locked the doors and looked up, there was the muzzle of a .38 Special pointed right at my head through the pane of the glass door. When I looked him in the eyes, something seemed to rock back within him. He didn't pull the trigger and instead ran away. The Lord had heard my prayer—I dropped to my knees with a sigh of relief and the sign of the cross.

Six years later, I was running the family liquor store in Newark, New Jersey while also attending college. Newark at the time was one of the country's most dangerous cities, and between my uncle Ambiorix and cousin Jhon Pipe, we operated the liquor store. We were all around 19 years old back then learning to run and operate a liquor store in a tough neighborhood. It was our trial by fire, learning how to perform well under pressure. And there was a lot of pressure; from the day-to-day business operations to dealing with the neighborhood thugs, and temptations with the endless hours behind the counter. Sometimes as people were paying for their six-pack and pint of whiskey, their "goods" would drop on the counter either by accident or as a test. Either way, they wanted to see our reaction. Would we say something? Look them in the eye? Push it away? Get *shook-scared*? Or just pick up the bills and loose change making sure not to touch anything else. We collected the money and nothing more.

Every now and then, we'd get invited or offered a free sample, just like when the big corporate reps come by to introduce a new product. Always turning down the offer.

We came to know everybody who came through our doors, but we were also deaf, dumb and blind towards anything that didn't pertain to our business. I came to see that the game played in Newark was just like the one in Harlem where we saw the preppies being traded like baseball cards by the corner boys. You would see the college kids or business people fall into the same trap. We lived with the Lord's Prayer on our lips because at any given time, anything could set them off. And in many of our compatriots' places, it did with many losing their lives. For us, it was survival inside and outside those iron gates. *Clack, clack, clack!* the gates went up every day and down at night; two of us looking out while the other locked up.

Although my business education partly came from sitting behind a desk in a lecture hall, but mostly it came from the store aisles. It would be funny to listen to some of the professors talking about running a business when most didn't have the slightest idea. By the time I graduated, I already had 10 to 12 years' experience managing a business in the real world.

Life Lesson

Learn from the tough situations of others and your own. Recognize all the blessing that you have and let them fuel you to rise up and grow. Maintain an attitude of gratefulness while using daily prayer to strengthen your resolve.

8
Corozo - Life on a Farm

During our elementary school years from the day that school got out, Mom and Dad would send us back home to our grandparent's farm in Corozo, Dominican Republic. Corozo is a small town with great fertile land in the mountainous region of the Dominican Republic known as "El Cibao." It's about 60 minutes away from the second biggest city on the island, Santiago de los Caballeros.

We only came back a day or two before the start of the new school year. Every summer, it seemed like we met more and more cousins, uncles, aunts, and extended relatives. With dirt roads, no electricity or running water, Corozo was a little kid's playground dream. We had lizards to catch, chickens to chase that would later become our dinner, and a cool river to swim in. We were far removed from the world. We were little kids carrying small knives to cut up mangoes we just picked or avocados grabbed from a neighbor's tree that just so happened to hang over our side of a fence. We played tag on the river banks and watched in awe during the heavy rain season when the river would swell, carrying away anything in its path from entire trees to live cows. Everywhere we went, there were family members to look after us because as it turned out, we really are all related. Dominicans everywhere have a joke that we are all connected, all family, and it's why most of us call each other Primo or Prima (cousin) upon meeting one another.

While the older kids worked in the fields or took odd paying jobs in neighboring towns, we kids got to explore everywhere. We would get our chores done early after getting up with the first rooster's crow. Then we'd brush our teeth and freshen up deep inside the coffee grove or next to a palm tree, using an old coffee can or jar to hold the water. By then Grandma would have the fire *del fogon* (clay fire pit) going that made the pots jet black on the outside. She would be making coffee over the open fire and the kids would get a cup with some casave, just like the adults, or maybe some bread to share among all of us.

There was only one kid in town, Leseito, who had a bike— it was a 10-speed with skinny tires and all which wasn't the best type of bike for riding on dirt paths. He only took it out on Sundays after church where everyone wore white. After mass, he would rent out his bike: five spins around the field that we played baseball in for five cents. Dad would give my uncles and I (my uncles and I were all the same age) twenty-five cents each so that we could each get five spins on the bike. It was simple, innocent fun and sometimes we would dart down one of the paths to take an extra-long ride on the last spin. We would go past the church and come back to the baseball field where Leseito would tell us that he would never rent us the bike again for taking it on such a long ride.

The houses in Corozo were all made of wood planks with tin roofs and polished dirt floors that when wet would be slipperier than any ice skating rink. All the boys slept in the same room with no door between the room with all girls. Our grandparents slept in their own room. Every night at bedtime, we all would fall asleep while talking and telling stories in the dark. We all made sure not to drink or eat too much before going to bed because no one wanted to walk the 100 yards away to the outhouse in the middle of the night.

One of my favorite things was listening to the sound of the rain hitting the tin roof, which would echo around the entire house. When there was lightning and thunder, my grandmother would throw a blanket over the only two mirrors in the entire house. It was something I never quite understood but I think she feared that maybe uncovered mirrors would attract lightning. We would collect as much rainwater as we could in barrels so that in the morning we would not have to head down the river to get the day's water supply. The best was when we were allowed to play under the rain sprouts, kicking up mud and cleaning ourselves up.

As soon as our chores were done, my uncles and I would leave to explore. We were all around the same age with maybe a year or two between us all. It was Fausto, Jose Luis, Ambriox, who we still call Cao until this day, and me plus my cousins Jhon Pipe, Dennis and Herlin. We would meet up on one of the dirt paths and head into the arroyos to catch frogs or collect pomos, which were half-dollar sized seeds that grow near the river or arroyos - streams and we'd make whistles out of them.

We always left with a knife or two and a couple of sacks to carry back home our bounty from our raids into other fields. We'd have to make sure not to get caught up in the barbed-wire fences, but almost always one of us would end up ripping a shirt or shorts and cutting ourselves too - the blood then attracting every single mosquito in the area. We would set out to hike the different trails and wherever we found a tree ripe for picking, we would raid it and eat our fill from the top of its branches. We would then collect as much as we could to carry back home. The best climbers were probably Cao and Jose Luis, with Jhon Pipe and I catching the mangoes or avocados that they tossed from the tree tops. Inevitably, we always found our way back home around lunch time and would have to sneak some of our bounty into the store room because my grandmother would not be too happy to find sacks full of fruit that we took for ourselves from someone else's land. We always hid some for an afternoon snack or to take with us to the river where we went swimming. I remember once we carried a sack full of ripe bananas "un racimo de gineo" into the store room and were looking forward to having them later that day. We came back later only to find every last one of them gone. It seemed that everyone who passed by the storeroom grabbed a few to eat for themselves. Since there were more than 15 people living in the house, those bananas didn't last very long.

Probably the most fun I had was walking lizards on leashes. Fausto taught us how to make a slip knot from a tall piece of grass. Next, we would quietly and patiently slip it over one of the seemingly millions of lizards that were always around. As the lizard got spooked, he would jump and get caught in the slip knot. As it tightened, you'd then have a lizard on a leash. Just imagine a bunch of seven to 10-year-olds walking around with lizards on leashes. The women in the family didn't really appreciate it much when we brought our pets into the house and would kick us out. But still, being curious ruled the day and learning to make something from nothing enhanced our creativity.

I learned to swim in the Amina river that runs through our little village by being thrown off the highest rock in "el charco prieto" (the dark watering hole) by my uncle Rolando. He would only dive in after me when I didn't come back up for air and when the current carried me a few yards away. I could imagine if my mother had seen this method of teaching her son to swim how she probably would have put a stop to it and never let me back out with the boys to explore the world. But I guess she never found out because it was how Billy and Maggie learned how to swim too. Getting thrown into the river and having just enough adrenaline, survival skills, craziness, and fun to learn how to swim in the rapids.

After our swim in the mornings we still had more chores to do. Our chores included separating the calf's from the mom so that there would be milk to collect in the morning feeding the pigs or corralling any that happened to get loose. You have no idea how fast a 200-pound pig can run and out maneuver a bunch of 10-year-olds! A lot of times we would just have to tire the pig out to get him back into its pen. The worst was when one of the perfectly white rabbits got out of its cage and fell into the school outhouse. There was no way we were going to let him stay there and so we spent the afternoon trying to get him out with a rope. We finally caught him in the noose and heaved him up the hole. I can still smell him now. Although terrible, we were heroes for the day!

For me, spending my summers on my grandfather's farm in Corozo are some of my best memories of my childhood. Sitting under the night sky with all the stars out, eating sugar cane from out back that my grandfather Pachu would peel and cut with the machete that never left his side. Everyone telling stories and jokes, passing the time away before we all went to bed where more jokes and stories would be told.

Life Lesson

Look back to your past and recognize how far you've come. Relish the history of what was, but realize that the past is the past to be enjoyed in beautiful memories and not to languish in. Think back to when you were a kid full of energy and curiosity - what did you love to do? Who was instrumental in your life? What lessons from then do you still use today? Which memories will you share now with your own family?

9
Games We Played

As boys let loose in the countryside, we found ways to keep ourselves entertained. We'd find and collect old motorcycle tires to race one another, making a wooden handle out of the bark of a palm tree (with a spatula-like end) to help steer the tire. We'd then race each other through our own makeshift obstacle course, pushing the tire in front of us, while using the big wooden paddle to steer and eventually crash into one another. Our legs were the engine while we made motorcycle sounds with our mouths. Years later, as I was giving a tour to my wife and kids, I bumped into a little boy racing ahead of his mother on one of the most remote paths. He must've been about six years old and I froze in my tracks with a huge smile on my face. I pointed to my kids to watch the little boy race up and down the path dodging chickens and branches with the expertise of a real motocross rider. Finally, my kids were able to see how and what I played with as a kid. As we neared the boy and his mom I asked, "Amiguito pudiera yo manejar su motor?" (My little friend can I get a ride on your motorcycle?) With a wide grin he hands me the wooden paddle and an old motorcycle tire. For 10 minutes, I ran up and down the dirt path we were on. His mother must've been thinking, "what is a grown man doing playing with little boys' toys?" My kids and wife were laughing at me, trying to keep the tire rolling and upright. Obviously I was out of practice, but I had a new friend running beside me, offering me tips on how to control "the bike."

Not having any toys didn't stop us from getting creative. I remember we made cars and trucks out of tin cans. We'd use the small cans of Victorina Tomato Sauce as wheels and an old oil can as the truck's body. These rides had to be seen. We attached a piece of rope made of guano (palm leaves) to pull behind us as it rattled and jumped its way across the rocky paths. There wasn't a Nintendo, Xbox, nor electricity, so we made up our games.

Today nearly all the homes in Corozo have running water, electricity, the Internet and all the modern appliances. However, Mom and Dad still like to keep the farm house a bit disconnected from the outside world by cooking and eating every meal outside under the big mango tree. During the mango season, one still needs to watch out and avoid a falling one-and-a-half-pound mango from hitting your head.

Life Lesson

Be resourceful. Get creative. Let your imagination carry you away. Figure it out and do not focus on what you do not have. Open your eyes and recognize how much you've got.

10
A Quarter Earned

Dad definitely believed in child labor and had us working from a young age. Although he never paid us, he showed us how we could make money working for tips. So that at 10 years old, we were already experts at serving our neighbors, making a few dollars through tips while bagging groceries and making deliveries. It was always enough for a slice of pizza and soda with enough left over to play some arcade games like Pac-Man and Centipede.

Saturdays were the best days. It seemed like everyone went grocery shopping on Saturday. I would set myself up at the busiest register lane, helping the cashier polish the counter, refilling the bag carrier and prepping all the bags so as soon as the cashier scanned the items and passed them to me, they were packed away. Most importantly, I never forgot my tip cup with a few coins and a dollar in it to entice neighbors to drop in their change rather than put it away inside their purse.

Sometimes some of the local kids, or the butcher's son would come in to bag too. We'd compete to see who was able to get the most tips and bag the fastest and the best. There is an exact science to properly bagging groceries. Back then we bagged everything in paper bags and one plastic bag. Cereal boxes would go toward the outside corners along with cans in order to properly balance the weight so the bag wasn't too heavy to carry. You never put the laundry detergent with the produce. Everything was to be sorted and separated. All frozen and refrigerated items went together helping them stay cold on a hot summer day. Plus, it made it easier for families to unpack at home and organize their pantry. Doing all this correctly and quickly got them thinking of you as they unpacked everything. Doing a great job bagging earned you more tips and therefore more money. The mom shopping with her husband and kids would pick your lane because you knew how to pack her bags and let her get her groceries home safely without the risk of her goods toppling over in the middle of the street, or worse—down the stairs of their walk-up apartment. I hustled for every quarter I got - nickels, dimes, and pennies too. It didn't matter to me because anything dropped in my cup got me closer to a dollar bill. Every dollar bill got me closer to a five-dollar bill, then a ten-dollar bill and hopefully a twenty-dollar bill.

Making twenty dollars bagging and doing deliveries was not an easy task. It meant standing on your feet all day, minimal breaks, keeping the counter clean and motivating the cashier to scan quickly and efficiently by buying her a cup of coffee or snack. You had to help upload the shopping cart for the mom who was juggling a baby and a toddler that was pulling at her leg. You were making sure to smile, say hello, and thank them whether they dropped something in your cup or not.

Making deliveries is where you really were able to make a few dollars. This involved - filling up a shopping cart with a neighbor's groceries packed in boxes, walking to their building, and loading box after box on your shoulder to climb the four or five stories up. I didn't care if it was one block or ten. Just like the mailman neither rain, sleet or snow was going to prevent me from my mission to collect as many dollars at a time as I could by doing deliveries. I would not only walk 10 blocks and carry them up five flights of stairs, but would also ask if they wanted me to unpack them, laying everything down on the small counters and kitchen table by category. If I noticed a bag full of empty bottles ready for redemption worth five cents each, I'd politely ask if they wanted me to take them and get them out of the way. But I'd only ask after they gave me my tip so as to not risk being shortchanged.

But some days were better than others. The worst was when I attracted the attention of the corner boys and they would steal my cart full of groceries, empty my pockets, and clock me in my head or shove me to the ground. They would run away laughing, only leaving behind a cloud of funny smelling smoke. I'd run back to the store, holding back tears in my eyes from having gotten mugged again. Dad would give me a couple of dollars to get a slice of pizza and soda while we waited for the neighbor to call and complain about why her groceries hadn't been delivered. I would explain to her what happened, pack her order, and get sent right back out to deliver her groceries again.

It became a game to those boys. Sometimes they took the whole cart, sometimes just whatever was in my pockets, and sometimes everything. Every block had its own set of corner boys. If I got past one group, I had to deal with another. I had to figure out different routes to take, or take a partner with me, which eventually meant splitting up the tips and even that didn't guarantee we wouldn't get jacked.

Other days were just as bad; hustling for tips, doing your best bagging and not making very much. My brother Billy still remembers being about nine years old and working all day from opening to closing bagging groceries and making deliveries but only making one quarter the entire day--just 25 cents! Being only nine, he didn't understand. He did everything right, worked hard, helped out, greeted everyone and said thank you but he didn't make any money. Dad, seeing that he was upset, took him aside and explained to him that on some days you can do everything right and still not make what you think you deserve. He also told him to not forget the days where he made more than he expected. Either way, you still have to show up and do the work. Dad still didn't pay Billy, just reinforced that next time he had to be just a bit better. He would have to hustle a little harder.

Life Lesson

Sometimes no matter how hard you work at something, you do not get the desired result. Keep at it. Do not quit. Everything takes time and effort but only you can put in the time and effort to make create something. No one else can do it for you.

Part Two:
Lessons From My Father

Raised As One

By a father who is more like our brother

Who taught us courage, love, honesty, and loyalty

Brothers raised to be men

Raised to be fathers

Instilled in us

No bond stronger than family

No love greater than our own

Respect held high

Maintained through humility

Sons of a shoe shiner

Who dreamed greater than most

With calloused hands pushing us

Forward

Never in his pocket

Strapped to a rocket to the moon we shot

Our feet to the ground but eyes to the sky

We've grown as he wished and should be proud of him as he is of us

To me you are as much brother as you are my father

11
The Backbone and The Bull

My father dropped out of school at third grade and Mom at fifth grade. Growing up in a Dominican Republic's farming community meant being isolated from any major city by mountains and without accessible roads to the nearest city. They were needed at home to work and school was a long ways away. But thankfully through the help of family and friends, they were able to learn to read and write whereas many others did not get the same privilege. My mother worked helping her parents with all her brothers and sisters *guyando yucca para hacer casave* (grating cassava roots to make casave bread). Papi did everything from being the local errand boy, hustling to be the best shoe shiner around, and milking the cows for one of his neighbors. Until this day, Dad can't stand anything made with milk because as he was milking, he would kill his hunger pangs by squirting the milk directly into his mouth before filling the can of milk for the owner.

My dad didn't have a father who cared for or nurtured him. His older brother, Pachango, took on that role of father and far exceeded it. They were brothers with the same mother, but different fathers. Pachango even gave Dad his own last name, changing it from Azcona to Estevez, solidifying the bond between them. This bond is so strong, even today, that no one would dare try and break it. I hope to have one such as theirs with my own brothers and sister. Once married, Pachango took Dad to live with him and loved him like a son.

Dad, never being fully clear of who his true father was, had Pachango's love to help fill the void. Pachango taught Dad everything he would need to know about life, running a business, and being a man. Most importantly, through his love and respect, he taught Dad about being a father. He pushed Dad as hard as he pushed himself, growing together in more ways than one and continuing to do so today. They both still hold each other accountable to looking for opportunities, and with a strong desire to "traer algo a la mesa" (bring something to the table).

Within his little country town and all around neighboring ones too, Pachango was larger than life. At around seven years old, he started with one burro (donkey), putting himself to work and renting out his lone donkey to carry loads. Back then, there were no roads just single-track trails. Their town Corozo was hidden deep in the mountains with fertile farmlands but with little to no access to the bigger towns that were farther away.

Pachango figured out that the isolation of Corozo was his opportunity. Only a kid, he was already thinking like a man. At dawn, he set out to the larger towns after loading his burro with the fruits, vegetables, casave, and anything else he was able to get from his neighbors. Whatever he sold he'd get to keep a portion of the profits and returned everything that was left over. So just like Sir Richard Branson of Virgin Atlantic, he protected his downside by taking on the calculated risk of venturing out with products of others to sell.

But Pachango had bigger plans. While in the big city, he used his profits to buy things that were needed back on the farm. He'd make an even bigger profit selling the merchandise along the way back home. Saving everything in a matchbook box, he reinvested it in his little business so that by the time he was 12 years old, he had more than a dozen burros in his caravan.

Eventually the government and a nearby lumber mill scratched out a crude road wide enough for a truck to get in and out of the lumber mills. The road was still too far away for most, but it crossed directly across Pachango's path into the big city. Again, he saw an opportunity. The truckers would sometimes bring goods to sell along the way making a few extra bucks for themselves. What if he did not have to make the full round trip to the city and back? Instead, he'd place an order with a friendly trucker who didn't mind making a few extra pesos to carry rice, beans, pottery, tools, and anything else for the kid with the caravan of donkeys. Doing this saved Pachango time, energy, and money because he would not have to carry the goods as far on his donkeys anymore. On top of that, he would be able to carry some loads from the mills to the trucks.

He learned the times when the truck loaded and unloaded. Pachango slept in the fields with his dozen or so donkeys right next to where the lumber trucks turned around. It was either sleeping with his donkeys under the stars or risking the chance of someone else getting their caravan hired. He hustled day and night. Whenever the trucks were there, he was there loading, unloading, buying, and selling. Then packing everything up, he went selling farm door to farm door.

He kept a strict account of everything and was fair with everyone. He was trusted and rose to become a leader in the community although he was still a boy.

Little by little, he kept adding pieces to his business. He bought a small piece of land, and harvested mani (peanuts), batata, and yucca. He eventually built a bodega in his hometown and taught my father how to buy and sell. It's because of these lessons from Pachango, that Dad is the man he is today.

My father could probably best be described as a compassionate bull. He is strong, determined and focused - able and willing to ram through barriers and breakdown walls either with sheer brute force or by outworking you. But, at the same time, he is compassionate--always showing love and respect and lending a helping hand to anyone who needs it. He gave second and third chances to people, even when he was burned by them more than once. I believe that his willingness to go the extra mile to help someone and show them that it's OK to make mistakes, as long as you learn from them, was because of the people who gave him a second chance. He believes that people should be given the benefit of the doubt and be encouraged to do better. In his own tough love way, he made all those around him better. He never has tried to portray himself as an angel - probably more as a man just trying to make the best out of the circumstances before him. He never listened or cared about gossip, and never held any grudges. Mami would tell me, "el *no les da mente a que ya a pasado solo como vamos a progresar*" – he never thinks of the past only how to move forward. One of Morel's greatest skills is being able to move forward in spite of whatever challenge may be thrown his way. He showed us his mistakes, stood up to them, and faced them showing us his errors in judgement. He asked of us to learn from them so that we would not repeat the same mistakes that caused him pain and suffering, but also gave us the freedom to fail. He never said to us "you see, if you just listened," but, instead, let us gain the experience from our failures. He always reminded us when we were each at our most rebellious points that "*uno siempre tiene que tener a alguien quien respetar*" - you must always have someone who you respect and look up to. Even if we would not listen to him, we always needed to have someone to look up to and respect and ask for guidance when things got tough. Without that, you will never be able to learn from your mistakes and grow to who you want and deserve to become.

When Dad was really putting in a lot of hours at the bodega or dealing with seemingly insurmountable pressure, the only person who was able to soothe him was Mami. She was able to help him see what was before him and through her support, prodding, nurturing, and praying, she encouraged him and guided us. Mami truly has been the backbone of our family, keeping us unified. Dad would tell us there should never be anyone greater than your mother. Always hold her in high respect because apart from your own children, your mother is the most sacred thing you will ever have in your lives next to God.

As young kids, we went to bed before Dad came home. We got up and ready for school and he was already gone. The only proof of him ever having come home were the groceries sitting on the table, still in their brown paper bags. Dad worked and worked and worked we rarely got to see him at home. Many times Mom would prepare dinner and walk us over to la bodega on the corner of 172nd Street and Audubon, the one with the yellow safety bars next to the convent. She did this so we could have dinner together as a family in the back room that was used for storage. Mom would arrange big boxes of paper towels to make a makeshift table and turned over milk crates for us to use as chairs. Then she would lay out the food just as if we were at home, with plates, utensils, and napkins. She was determined that we ate as a family. Even the bodega cat, Mishu, would join us for dinner, rubbing against our legs, waiting for one of us to drop a few grains of rice while we ate.

While Dad was working 16 to18 hours a day, Mom was taking care of us and him; making sure that we remained a family. She taught us to never forget our roots, to be humble, and to respect and keep God present in our hearts. Mom has shown us that compassion, love and a prayer can do so much not only for ourselves, but also for those around us. She worked so very hard helping others. We have a running joke and tease her a bit that we cannot make money fast enough for her to give it away. She spends most of her time building houses, feeding and clothing the poor, repairing churches and doing outreach for those less fortunate. Sometimes it can get a little nutty, but Mom's heart is in a great place. She reminds us that we come from nothing and it is our privelege to always contribute back. To this very day, we support the local churches near our stores by keeping their food banks replenished and helping with fundraising drives. It's just another small way to support our neighbors.

Life Lesson

Respect the effort of others and what they have done. Take a minute from your day to thank your parents, family, team, or a veteran. People feel good when someone recognizes their effort - let them know how much you appreciate what they've done and how it has positively affected you.

12
Trouble Shows Up

This is a story that I have only heard in bits and pieces. My own siblings don't really know the details. It is just whispered around like a rumor and it was about my father. It bugged me for years and I never had the courage to ask him directly. But it was a story I had to hear for myself to clear up the doubts. The thing about it was people from everywhere revered him for it, but he never ever spoke about it. He just wanted to bury it inside him. I almost felt guilty for asking him to tell it to me, as tears immediately streamed from his eyes.

Speaking in almost a whisper Dad begins, "I was 15 years old. That problem arrived at our house. He was a soldier who had fought against the American invasion in 1965. He was a war veteran. He left Corozo and joined the army and lived in the capital city. But when he felt like it, he came back into town with his M16 machine gun and he would be drunk all the time. He'd force the bodega owners to give him all the rum he wanted and anything else he could take away from them. Always threatening to kill the shop owners if they refused. Sometimes just for fun, he would shoot up all the shelves just to watch the bottles blowing up. He would be up on anyone and randomly would knock someone out for no reason. Unfortunately, for years and years he did this, leaving for the capital and coming back to terrorize everyone."

"But then one day he showed up at our house. Mama was taking a break from her cooking under a tree in our small yard. I was home and it was starting to get dark already. I was always home by nightfall like everyone else. We never had a problem at home or anywhere - we were never trouble makers. But that day, the soldier shows up.

His name is Jaime. He is still around now living full time in Corozo. I actually help him every now and again when I hear he needs something."

"But that day he shows up drunk at our house and I saw Mama dart away from where she was sitting and scream. The younger grand kids were in the kitchen having dinner. He flips the table over, throwing all the food to the ground and the kids with it. Then he dumped all the pots and began trashing Mama's kitchen. He would've attacked Mama but I rushed in, yelling at him as if he'd gone crazy."

"He slapped me down, but I got up and with all the rage inside me, I lost my senses. I just reacted and we began fighting, I was strong but he was a *soldier*. I wanted to get to the machete we used around the house and in the fields. I broke free and was running to where the machete was kept, but Jaime was gaining on me. I wasn't going to make to the machete. Jaime caught up to me and I grabbed "una mano de pilon" – a heavy pestle that we used to grind coffee. I was just 15 years old and he was bigger than me, but I grabbed la mano de pilon. I was always taught to respect anyone in uniform, especially the military, but he was attacking my mother, trying to God knows what to her. And now he was attacking me."

"So I swung the mano de pilon and knocked him to the ground and just kept beating him with it. Then he stopped moving, stopped fighting back. I thought

I killed him. He had to be hospitalized for two weeks. I turned myself into the local deputy but they never locked me up. They let me go home and kept watch over me, waiting to see whether Jaime would live or die. It was the scariest part of my life - that fight and what came after it. Pachango was already in New York so I had no one to stand up for me or to guide me. I had never been in trouble before and didn't know what to do."

"But the big problem came when he was released from hospital - he came after me with his brother, who was a soldier too. I had to go into hiding because they were hunting me down. I was living and eating in the fields. Everyone in town was scared. I hid in the fields and farms away from everyone and everything. Their threats kept escalating, but now the men in town were standing up and keeping a close eye on them, ready for anything. The neighbors stood up for me. During that time, one of the town's elders, Pachu rallied up more men and let it be known he would be responsible for me and any actions. Pachu declared to be my protector and that if anything were to happen to me, they would have to answer to him. Pachu was well-respected in town. He was a family man who was building his own legacy. Only when he spoke up and sent word for me did I come out of hiding and from then on, he took me under his wing. I became a son to him and he gave me the stability of a home. I joined his family and was accepted in the fold as one of his own. Things settled down a bit after Jaime's brother left and he remained living on the outskirts of town, having been discharged from the army. But still he couldn't let things be and tried to attack me on one of the local paths. I held him back throwing rocks at him.

Someone went into town and told them what was happening and 30 men showed up, chasing him back home. They made it very clear that he would no longer terrorize anyone again pulling up each and every fence stake around his property. People began to feel safe."

"Later, word spread that Jaime had been beaten and was no longer a threat. I wasn't proud and I never spoke about it until now because you brought it up. I was scared - I had almost killed a man by defending my mother and myself. The only good thing that came from that was gaining Pachu as a father figure. He became your grandfather."

Dad holds no grudges. Pachango did go speak to him on a trip he had made back home from New York, letting him know that even though Jaime did attack the family, that we should stop all bad blood between him.

"But you have to imagine," he said.

Anyone who enters your home, what choice do you have? You have to do whatever you can to stop them from hurting your family. That problem arrived at our doorstep and we were not looking for trouble. That's the only problem I've ever had in life. I'm not proud of it and wish it never happened. Even today I will continue to help him in any way possible."

Life Lesson

Always be ready to fight for what you believe to be right. Stand up, speak up, say or do something. You have the power to correct a wrong and make things right. Just be vigilant that you heart remains pure, hold no grudges and always be willing to forgive.

13
Bodegueros

Sometimes the phone would ring at 1:00 a.m. and it would be Cheo, the old Cuban that worked in the bodega with my father. Dad came by after closing the supermarket to check on the bodega. There would always be a few guys playing dominoes on the sidewalk or talking about the Yankees game. Dad would then have a few beers with them to unwind. He had already worked a full day in the supermarket, getting up at 5:00 a.m. to unload the grocery trucks. His second shift at the bodega was from 9:00 p.m. to closing, but now that he had his childhood best friend, Niño, tending to the bodega, he really didn't have to be there on a constant basis. But Dad would go to let off steam and have a few beers with the guys, sometimes ending up having one too many. Anytime this happened, Cheo would call the house usually at closing to arrange for someone to pick up dad. Then Mami would wake John and I up and we'd drive across the George Washington Bridge to the 190th Street Bodega to pick him up.

John, who only had his permit, double parked the car outside the bodega and headed inside to get Dad to drive him home. By now, closer to 2:00 a.m. all of the bodega gates were pulled down except the entrance gate, which is only half way down, so we slide under. We knocked and Cheo would let us in. Here we were, two kids, pushing through a cloud of cigarette smoke past the drunk men slamming down dominoes. We begin to convince them to break up their domino game by soothing, cajoling, and conning them that it was time to go. None of them wanted to leave so we would entice them with another cold one on the sidewalk. Leaving Cheo to lower the gates, we slipped away as they cracked opened their beers. Sliding Dad onto the front seat, we drove back, knowing full well that we had to get up for school by 7:00 a.m. At home we would undress him and lay him to bed, making bets with each other that he wouldn't get up to open the store. But sure enough, before we got up, Dad would be gone and ready to work.

An unfortunate constant that surrounded bodegueros life was fighting. Whether fighting in the street by local school kids, thugs, or anyone else, tempers always seemed to flare short within the neighborhood. Every week there was one or two big battles that you would witness or hear about just around the corner. My fights tended to be on the more innocent side but I didn't see it like that back then. Every time I visited dad at the bodega I would get into a fight with, a kid, who lived down the block. On sight, he and I would go at it throwing fists in air. Sometimes he caught me restocking the milk in the back corner and would jump me from behind. Other times I would see him coming through the door and rush him into the potato chip rack. Dad, watching from behind the counter, and his father were the referees. They allowed us to fight, sometimes even enticed us to fight. I guess it was their way of toughening us up for the real fights that would come in our later years. Eventually someone would separate us and have us clean up the mess we made followed by a **Life Lesson**. It was OK for us to want to protect ourselves, but we needed to learn to be friends. Fighting should only be a last option. But we didn't hear what they were telling us and continued to fight every day that summer.

While my fighting was a bit more docile, John had his own nemesis who would come into the store causing trouble, trying to bully who he could, and taking what he wanted. Every day John or one of the other guys had to grab him and forcibly remove him from the store. Things kept escalating each time he came in and each time he was thrown out. This day was no different and the guy kept coming back over and over again. Eventually, the guy called John outside. See, he had already planned that this was not going to be a fair fight, that he was going to get the upper hand and make John pay for all the humiliation he went through for constantly being kicked out of the bodega. They begin to fight, John again with the advantage. As expected, the guy reached for a knife he had hidden, but it wasn't there. As Dad was driving up in the bodega van, he saw where the guy hid a knife between the iron gates and took it away. Again, the guy is beat and kicked off the block by John.

The next morning as John and Dad are throwing up the iron gates, they find out that the troublemaker John fought the day before was killed by someone else that got tired of him. It made them realize that John's fight could have gone a lot differently. What if John had gone too far or if Dad had not pulled up just at the right time to see the guy hiding the knife? Things changed and happened fast in our neighborhood.

It was always like this in the bodega - a million things going on at once. The old Cuban Cheo would keep me behind the counter with him as he would run the calculator, grind a pound of coffee, sell a pack of Marlboro Lights and Double Mint gum, pop a beer bottle open and stick it in a brown paper bag for a guy to guzzle down before stepping outside. I'd load a merengue cassette to play over the speakers as the chatter in the store was relentless. It was where everyone met up at after work to get the last few items to cook, moms sent their kids on an errand to pick up a couple of plantains and dads threw back a few cold ones before heading up the five flights of stairs to watch the Yankees. Where you heard the latest gossip, got all your groceries and met everyone in the neighborhood. It was where the local beat cop would go on his bathroom break and chug a beer in the back before heading back into the New York City heat. Where one mom's stroller would cause a traffic jam in the narrow aisles trapping all the other shoppers between a mountain of platanos (plantains) and an ice chest filled with Heineken's todas vestida de novia (all ice cold and frosted). The bodega was the lifeblood of the city block, the connection back to the Dominican Republic where you could learn what was happening back home, pick up some of your favorite brands from the DR and find out what company was hiring downtown. Guys yelled "capicua" as they slammed down the dominoes, kept a pint under the table and taking sips while the pieces got shuffled.

The summertime was the busy season for bodegas as people couldn't stand being stuck inside their hot apartments and would spend a good amount of time after work hanging outside their building stoop. Grabbing a bag of chips, soda, and sandwich for the kids and maybe a six-pack for mom and dad to share with their neighbors. Dad knew that people would be making more trips into the bodega and having the coldest beer around would be a draw. People would walk a few extra blocks just to get a beer that was frosted over. We would pack the walk-in box fridge from floor to ociling with every case of Heineken, Becks, Bud and Miller we could. Then we'd fill garbage cans with ice and load them up with beer. We'd get it all ready for the after work rush knowing that on a scorching New York City day customers would pay extra for a frosted beer - que estaban ceniza!

Ever the one to drum up more business, on a few weekends a month all summer long, Dad would get anyone who knew how to play the drums, guira, accordion and could sing merengue and bachata to set up outside the bodega, pushing the domino players down the block. That rag tag group would play for a couple of dollars and all the cold beer they could drink. It brought everyone out of their apartments, dancing on the sidewalk, and those that didn't come down from their apartments would be looking out the window yelling out requests from their fifth floor perch. Chorolo y Su Combo would play merengue into the night. We'd sell out every cold bottle from the ice chest, our makeshift garbage can coolers, and the ice box. We literally dominated those summers with the music and ice cold beer. The hook to get more people through the doors. People soon spread the word that at the 190th Street bodega, a block party was going on and we were happy to serve them all.

Life Lesson

Become part of the community and contribute. Learn the different nuances of those you are serving and know that there are more people wanting to see you succeed than those that don't. Build strong ties and become an ally to your community.

14
House on a Hill

When Dad first came over to the United States from the Dominican Republic, like almost every Dominican coming over, he landed in Washington Heights. Washington Heights was fast becoming the capital for all things Dominican to the newly arrived. Located in Upper Manhattan with the George Washington Bridge connecting New Jersey and New York City, you could find everything a Dominican needed without ever leaving the neighborhood or speaking a word of English. It was such a big part of Dominican history for those who came to the U.S. Many even saying "I'm going to New York" as if it was a totally separate place than the United States of America. It was home away from home.

It was 1971 and Mom was already here. Her father, Simeon Rodriguez, my grandfather was one of the first Dominicans to come over from the island, along with my uncle Pachango. Soon after arriving, Dad began working in a factory in Hackensack, NJ just a short bus ride over the George Washington Bridge from Washington Heights. Many of the people from the neighborhood, and Dominicans from all over, worked there. But Dad never really liked the environment inside a factory - the gossip, repetition, and not having control. Pachango had risen to become the foreman without knowing a word of English nor how to read or write. Dad and Pachango had leadership skills and Pachango found himself in the old German supervisors' good graces. But they knew factory life was not for them.

In order to escape the gossip and idle chit chat, Dad would leave the factory on his lunch break and walk around the neighborhood. The factory was not too far from Hackensack's Main Street which was lined with shops, restaurants, and had that old time feel. This was the vibrant Main Street before the mall era took over our highways and suburbs. Hackensack's Main Street was the place to shop, eat, and have a stroll on. More and more, Dad began walking the neighborhoods around the factory, walking further and further and discovering the single family homes, green grass, trees and open spaces. On his day off from the factory he would bring Mom, John, Maggie and I to walk on Main Street and get away from the Washington Heights where everyone lived on top of each other. Everything made of concrete, gray and rough. Hackensack gave him the vision of the open space back home in Corozo. Eventually on one of his long walks, Dad walked up the tallest hill in town. From the top you could see the New York City skyline and even on a clear day the Empire State building and the Twin Towers. From there he vowed to one day move his family to a house on that hill.

Little did he know that just about 10 short years later, we would be the first Dominicans to move into Hackensack from Washington Heights. Buying that house on a hill for what was, to him, all the money in world. I remember on so many nights after dinner we would walk out of our house, walk past three houses on our left, and look at the New York City skyline. Seeing the skyline from the same spot where Dad looked out and dreamed of one day owning a house when he first arrived to the States.

So many family members and friends tried unsuccessfully to convince my father not to buy a house and move to New Jersey. It was too much money. Too far away from family and friends. No other Dominicans are out there. Too dangerous for Dominicans. But no matter what they said, Dad knew that this was the perfect place for us to grow up, even though we were in New York City almost every day.

There were so many of us living under one roof. And as the first Dominicans to move to Hackensack, the transition for some was not as easy. The a few of the local residents really didn't like this new family that moved into their neighborhood. They didn't understand us. Why was a big old van, the one Dad used to carry groceries back and forth to supply his bodega, parked on our driveway? Why don't they speak English? What kind of people are always going into the city? Why do they leave so early and come home so late? How many people live there? We must have been a sight to see.

I remember that we went around introducing ourselves to a few of the neighbors, mostly just us kids. One particular family told us in not so kind words that they would put their house up for sale and move away unless we went back to where we came from. They moved away almost immediately. The father had a big thick mustache, a huge pot belly, and a cigar dangling from his face at all times of the day. He would randomly yell across the street whatever came to mind. But we didn't pay him any attention at all. One thing we learned quickly in our house was to adapt and do it quickly. Figure out what's going on, assess it, and take some sort of action. Don't worry about everyone else. Just worry about yourself and the family. We are here to work and move forward. And that's what we did.

One day after school, we heard our trash cans being turned over. There was yelling as the doorbell rang, and people banged on the doors. It turned out that all the local kids followed John home from school. John was around 13 years old. The other boys kept calling for him to come outside to fight. The kept calling us names and harassing us. We started to figure out that they were the same kids who knocked over our trash or stole all the food from the BBQ grill when Mom had run inside to get something. We never thought it was deliberate, just random things that were happening. But the kids kept chanting, banging on the doors, and lined up on the back edge of our yard.

At this point, John is ready to go out and fight. Mami, of course, tried to hold him back but knows that he will and must go outside to fight. So they both head out. Mami in her simple house dress, clutching a broom stick in her hands. John in shorts and a t-shirt. I watched everything from the kitchen window. They tried to jump him but Mom and John held them back. All the while John yelled "Come on, I fight you all!" One by one they started stepping up onto our red brick patio with all the other ones, yelling "kick his ass!" John was ready, picking each of them off - fighting some easier than the others. They were brawling and Mami was swinging her broom stick at any one who flinched and tried to jump in. I grabbed the rotary phone off the wall, dialing the bodega to get my father. I wanted him there now to stop the fighting and to make the boys go away. I was scared for John and for Mami. Some of these guys looked to be older than John and were high school kids.

The yelling outside was loud and constant.

Finally, Dad comes to the phone, having heard me frantic on the line yelling. I tell him there are 10 or 12 kids at the house yelling and screaming and cursing and fighting John. He asks me where Mami was and I told him she was outside "con un palo de escoba dandole a los tigres y John estas peliando" - with a broomstick hitting the other guys while John keeps fighting. I begin to give him a play-by-play from the window, stretching the cord of the wall phone completely to its limit. Dad stops me to ask "y John esta ganando?" - (is John winning?) I tell him yes! Then Dad says so let him keep fighting and hangs up the phone.

I watched in amazement as John took them out one by one. They finally scurried away like rats jumping into the gutters. John took some good hits, but he never dropped and kept fighting. Those kids never again messed with John or any of us. They didn't know that Dad had enrolled John in a boxing school, training not to be a boxer but to know how to defend himself. Living in Washington Heights and going to school there was rough. Even though he never had to fight there, he was tested in this seemingly calm beautiful neighborhood. We learned then "hay tigres en todo los lados" – there are tough guys everywhere and one had to be prepared.

Dad was used to fighting as he did so almost every day by stopping thieves or drug addicts or neighborhood bullies trying to steal from him. And anyway, to him, boys were supposed to fight and defend their home and their family. That night Dad came home a little bit early and was proud of John for being a man and protecting his family.

We happily lived in that house on a hill for a long time. So many people once again living under one roof: Me, Mom, Dad, John, Maggie, Billy plus my grandfather Pachu, my aunts Caridad, Angela and Anny, my uncles Juan, Rolando, and cousin Chamon. There were others coming and staying a few days at a time too. Everyone worked in the business. If anyone did move, others were welcome to stay with us, like my other uncles who are my age, Cao, Jose Luis, Negra, Jhon Pipe, Ramoncitio and his son. Our doors were always open. I slept on a queen sized bed with my two aunts until I was about 12 years old then finally got a bed of my own. We learned so much and ate in what seemed liked shifts. When the first wave arrived they ate, then the next, then the next. The conversations around the table and at every gathering was around business. Where to get the best meat, what vendor was caught stealing, who arrived late, who was doing a good job, what other bodega was doing well, and what was it that they were doing. The women and us kids would beg to change the subject to anything else. But it was always talking business. Dad would put us to use with his calculator that he always had in his pocket, calling out numbers and asking us to total them up, telling us to take out a percent and how to make a profit.

We would argue with him about how in school they taught us how to calculate a percent and then he would show us his way.

"Tho way they teach you In school, you won't make it a week in business." he said. "You have to understand there are expenses. Don't be fooled by vendors telling you or even showing you fancy tricks and numbers on their calculator. This is how you calculate a percent to make a profit. But always remember that the magic number is one hundred percent. So if you want to make forty percent gross profit on an item, divide the cost by 60. Go ahead, test it out with what they teach you in school and I bet you you'll make more money my way than what your teacher is telling you. Doing it my way you make a bit extra."

Over and over he would make us practice on the calculator, throwing real costs to real items of products we were selling. Then, taking away the calculators, he'd have us memorize the most common calculations and percentages in our head. Making sure it became second nature to us.

And as always, Dad was right.

Life Lesson

Make your vision greater than your desires. Let your vision propel you forward not allowing to be sway by others. Invest in the vision and share it with those that will help you achieve it.

15
On the Factory Line

Soon after beginning to work in the factory with Pachango, Dad, always hustling, bought himself a beat-up station wagon so that he could begin transporting his co-workers back and forth to the factory. This allowed him to boost his weekly earnings by twenty-five to thirty dollars. He was only making eighty-one dollars at the textile factory so the extra money really helped, especially with a growing family. By becoming the driver, he wouldn't have to pay for his own transportation, and he'd be making money on it instead. He figured out that getting a driver's license was the fastest way to earn a little extra cash. Mom worked at a nearby belt factory making only $75 per week. On a good week, they earned about $200 between their factory work and driving passengers back and forth. Their goal was to save $25 to $30 every week and they forced themselves to do it. They'd take on extra hours and always looked for other ways to make a little bit more and spend a little bit less than everyone else. Saving money and sending some money back home to Dad's mother every week created a habit of saving and building a foundation. Determined to get ahead, they worked hard by doing more than what they saw family and friends doing.

The linen factory where Dad worked was hard work. It required preparing linens in 15 yards, 20 yards, and 25 yards. They were prepping the materials for JCPenney, Macy's, and Sears. They shipped to every state and all kinds of places.

Dad was a fast learner. Eventually he was entrusted with the loading dock. It was a job that provided him with the experience which later became useful when he bought his first supermarket. Having managed the in and out flow of merchandise from the factory loading dock, he understood how important the back door receiving is to a business. Taking great care of the back door can make you or break you. It was important to make sure the right items were coming in at the right price and nothing was being taken out through the back door.

During this time, Pachango bought his first bodega and stopped working at the factory. Dad worked all day preparing linens and then dropped off his passengers, headed home to, eat and freshen up, and then right back to work at Pachango's bodega one block away. The bodega was a small place and needed a lot of work. It was nothing like the bodegas of today. Most were owned by Cubans and Puerto Ricans, but they were all really run down. The Dominicans changed the bodega business by providing fully stocked, clean, brightly lit stores, and offering additional services. In Washington Heights, Pachango was one of the first Dominicans to start in the bodegas and is considered a pioneer who paved the way for others. The bodega was perfect for Pachango since he was already an expert on buying, selling and procuring the items the neighborhood wanted. From the days of the donkey caravans, Pachango, honed his salesmanship skills. His boisterous, welcoming personality encompassed his bodega and it became the place for people to meet and to buy their favorite foods.

However, it was still a rough neighborhood with gangs and drugs everywhere and the bodega was right across from Highbridge Park. Highbridge Park was a favorite hangout of the gangs and Pachango didn't want his younger brother, my father, in that environment so he kept him away for fear of him getting into trouble. But Dad wanted to learn and even though Pachango sent him home, he would not leave. So he worked every night, alongside Pachango, learning everything about the bodega. Pay wasn't necessary because his motivation was helping his brother get ahead while learning as much as he could about being a bodeguero. Little by little, Dad was spending more and more time in Pachango's bodega. He eventually quit the factory telling Pachango "vamos echar esta viana pa'lante" (let's push this thing onward).

Dad was soon waking up at dawn to go to La Marketa to get supplies for the store. They split themselves up: Pachango tending to the counter and Dad getting supplies and keeping the store fully stocked. Both did anything and everything to make sure the bodega was operating at its best. They were young with a strong hustle gene. Soon the business started to grow. As the bodega really started to take off, their name and reputation grew with it. They were young and they put all that youthful energy into growing that single bodega. They wanted the bodega to evolve from a dingy store with sparse items to a mini mart, fully stocked up to the rafters. They changed what a bodega was and became a model for the New York City bodega that you would see popping up throughout the city.

Just as they were settling into a rhythm working the bodega, Pachango had to fly back down to the

Dominican Republic. His wife and kids were finally given visas and the family would be reunited. He entrusted the bodega to Dad while he was away.

With Pachango gone, it was time for Dad to prove himself. As Dad likes to say, "Ahi yo coji el mando!" (I took control). This was Pachango's bodega and he was determined to keep it growing while Pachango was in the Dominican Republic making the arrangements for his family to move to the States.

Dad believes the time spent working the bodega alone without Pachango was his true testing ground. It was where he learned to handle the pressure of countless hours that included buying, selling, and keeping the business alive. His motivation was that he wanted to make Pachango proud.

Months went by before Pachango returned with his family. Dad had passed the test! The bodega was thriving and they both fell right into cadence upon his return. Pachango couldn't have been more proud of his brother and reassured him that together they would continue to grow.

Soon after, Pachango bought another bodega that was for sale around the corner but this time he made Dad his partner. Now they had two bodegas within walking distance from each other. They began to dominate the neighborhood— leveraging the volume of both bodegas to get better deals to offer their neighbors.

Further accelerating their growth through their work ethic and creativity, they soon began to buy and flip bodegas throughout Washington Heights. They bought them cheap and fixed them up, using the same model they created on West 172nd Street. Their own bodegas became the training grounds for anyone that wanted to follow them into the bodega business. Working from 6:00 am to midnight, they made a name for themselves, eventually becoming the perfect example of the bodeguero.

I personally remember Dad's first bodega. I have a picture of him behind the counter hanging in my office. It was right next door to a convent. Now there was a clash of two cultures coming together on that New York City block! A wave of newly immigrated Dominicans replacing the Irish that lived there with the bodega being the center meeting point for everyone. Pachango and Dad were in the right place at the right time. It was the perfect launch pad into business: new faces arrived every day from the island who were under served and the bodegas became an opportunity to serve them.

Life Lesson

Be willing to put in the work. The work you are doing today is preparing for what is to come. Everyone would like to start off at the top not realizing that they may be ill prepared for what it takes to stay on top. Develop your skills so that you can take advantage of the opportunities to come.

16
Big Bet

As Dad began to go from the bodega business to the supermarket business, he was having a hard time getting a bank loan which he knew was be key in taking the next step to his evolution. He heard of other bodegueros going to one of the local warehouses who would loan money to anyone buying a store. The warehouse supplied all the groceries and in most the basic form, they would give you a promissory note. The note came at a very high interest rate, because they were taking a risk on you, but at the same time giving you the opportunity to grow. It really was how most of the independents grew; by borrowing from the warehouse to buy a supermarket. The two entities were co-dependent and happy to help one another.

The warehouse made money on the cost of goods, shipping, advertising, and loans. The store owners were given the opportunity to get a loan even if it was at a higher rate. Signing all types of guarantees in order to make an attempt to grow. The warehouse had the option to take over the business and then resell it to another operator in order to recoup their loss if the operator was not successful. But they never did lose. Instead, they'd resell the business and re-lend the money to another operator. The warehouses opened the door for Dominicans and many others to take over and become the major independent owners of New York City supermarkets. But that opportunity came at a cost. And it was probably why we as a group were labeled "Dumb Dominicans." Because at times money was borrowed from the warehouse, used irresponsibly. Some owners even used the same attorney as the warehouse - talk about conflict of interest! But when you are stepping up to a new level, sometimes the rules are not clearly explained and you just have to figure them out as you go.

This brings to mind the quote from Theodore Roosevelt: "It is not the critic who counts; not the man who points out how the strong man stumbles, or where the doer of deeds could have done them better. The credit belongs to the man who is actually in the arena, whose face is marred by dust and sweat and blood; who strives valiantly; who errs, who comes short again and again, because there is no effort without error and shortcoming; but who does actually strive to do the deeds; who knows great enthusiasms, the great devotions; who spends himself in a worthy cause; who at the best knows in the end the triumph of high achievement, and who at the worst, if he fails, at least fails while daring greatly, so that his place shall never be with those cold and timid souls who neither know victory nor defeat."

When Dad bought his second supermarket in Harlem he invited John in as a partner. John was studying accounting in a two-year community college and was just 21 years old. Digging into the numbers, John discovered some irregularities. And the more he dug, the more things didn't make sense. By that time, John urged Dad to hire a true accounting firm. He did and that's when the numbers began to tell their real story. The warehouse was tacking on a few extra points on the delivery and cost of goods, as well as making extra money on the advertising. The interest we thought were paying down turned out to be a different story as well.

Soon after, the questions and challenges began. John was labeled a troublemaker by the warehouse and they began advising all the other store owners to stay away from him. Saying that the Estevez family didn't know what they were talking about and were just causing trouble. John kept probing for answers and made friends with different vendors, people who had served the previous generation of supermarket owners who helped guide and educate Dad in the supermarket business. John and Dad made the conscious choice to take the steps to become bankable so that they could break free from the warehouse loans and their high rates.

With some in the industry, John was being portrayed as an agitator, an ungrateful entitled kid who would bring all that his father built to the ground. But the irony was John was right there building alongside Dad and we, the younger siblings would follow him. Before the break up, the heads of the warehouse called a meeting with Dad and were not too happy when father and son showed up. Dad had John's back. Even though they were stepping into unknown territory and all the other owner groups had been placated and would not move to a new co-op with us. Dad and John did their homework and knew well the story the numbers told. While the warehouse tried unsuccessfully to drive a wedge between Dad and John, they stood as one, just as always. Not an insult or bribe could separate them.

The warehouse did not like this because it meant a key revenue source was drying up. Fighting the warehouse was a bold move because they had the power to stop your deliveries, make them arrive late, help a "more friendly" competitor open up near you as punishment for challenging them. Many times, other operators called Dad or John advising them to listen, don't rock the boat, don't take this path, don't start a fight with the warehouse and think of our livelihood. Questioning their loyalty. Not realizing the loyalty was to the family and team. And to growing.

At the same time, a major New York bank started a lending program for small business owners that would bring together the bank and various supermarket groups. The program's liaison would learn the business from both sides and become the vehicle for supermarket owners and operators to become bankable. Having the bank's liaison on the operators' side who understood the nuances of lending, and were willing to learn how the warehouse structured their deals, helped us to become better businessmen. Growing these relationships helped many of us to move from being dependent on the warehouse to being bankable and enjoying true independence. A key shift for us came when John and Dad hired an accounting firm specializing in the supermarket industry. So now we had the beginnings of a true professional team working with us from accountants to bankers. Soon, a friendly attorney joined us that knew the ins and outs of the industry. These changes supercharged us and enabled us to go from single operator, renting our location, to landlords with multiple stores.

The day Dad paid the final note of his loan to the warehouse, he and mom got dressed up in their finest to mark the day. He cried tears of joy, thanking God for the opportunity and kissed the ground, saying over and over, "Now I can take the business anywhere."

John soon found out about the availability of a new store through our attorney. But the family was completely cash-strapped. Dad could not see how we would be able to buy a fourth store plus the building. But John and Dad wouldn't let go of the vision of owning the property. We were still fresh from fighting with the warehouse about its absurd interest rates and knew that going back to that watering hole was not an option. The only way to do it was flipping the smaller store on Metropolitan and using it as deposit.

Securing the first piece of property and paying off any remaining loans to the warehouse, along with setting up the right system and team, accelerated our pace. Although it took a lot of lot of work and sacrifice, it always came with the satisfaction of knowing we were working for ourselves. Our next evolution was going from working as an independent buying from the warehouse with no real advantage of the benefits of our efforts, to owning a piece of the business through the co-op model. So we went from bodegueros to independent supermarket retailer to co-op member with ownership interests. Each step helped us evolve, learn and grow. We used the lessons from each stage to propel us onto the next stage. At the co-op level, not only would we learn to work with other owners and a professional staff, but we would learn how to serve an even more demanding clientele. We would learn how to develop better merchandising, dig deeper into the number, and developing better strategies to gain an advantage in our neighborhoods. Whereas at the independent warehouse level, we were on our own. It served us well, but there's nothing like working towards a common goal with a team. Now we would be working to grow within the co-op. We immersed ourselves fully in the behind -the-scenes business, from advertising to case movements and placements. It is the perfect environment for a group, like us, that is always focused on growing and looking for what will push us *pa'lante* - onward!

Life Lesson

Know when to take on smart risks. Trust in your abilities. Aligned yourself with those who want to see you succeed. A key trait to have is learning to be comfortable in the uncomfortable. Knowing that true growth comes from the most difficult situations especially when you are pushing yourself towards them.

Part Three:
Lessons For Growth

A New Path

I'm the kid who grew up to be

A father of 3 – awesome kids

Who hasn't quite figured out

How he lucked out with such a great wife

Such a great life

I'm the kid who grew up

Between the aisles

Stocking up cans filled with dreams

I reached higher

S-T-R-E-T-C-H-I-N-G

To reach the top

Son of a shoe shiner

Who grew up behind the counter

Working iron hours

From the time the iron gates went up until they came down

Working side by side with my father and siblings

Starting from nothing

Building the foundation

I'm R-E-A-C-H-I-N-G

To make something

That takes me over the top

Puts me (us) in a new space

Level up

Into a new place

Come on let's set the pace

Face the challenge

New skills needed

Acquired

New capabilities

Required

Same work ethic obtained as a kid

Helps the man with the plan

Get the New deals coming

17
Making Friends

Just like in Hackensack, we found a great place to grow and expand. Taking a new location over in North Yonkers brought its own set of challenges. For one, we hadn't yet operated in a fully suburban style neighborhood with a middle class clientele. Learning the wants and needs of the neighborhood became our mission. Catering well to them was our goal. But almost immediately, rumors started swirling and lies began to spread. We were not going to be welcomed with open arms. It seemed that a few "didn't want those kind of people in the neighborhood." The irony being that the kind of people those few were talking about served their community, worked hard and honestly, and would bring a modern clean store into the neighborhood. But it didn't matter because as the rumors spread they were only delaying the inevitable.

For over two and a half years we were not allowed to do anything within the store mainly because we hadn't built up trust in the neighborhood. It was our job to let the neighbors get to know who we really were instead of them believing the rumors. The existing store was old, antiquated and full of health and safety violations. However, we couldn't fix any of it even though we were the rightful owners. We just couldn't get the permits. The neighborhood was clamoring for a new store to open, but it seemed like it was not meant to be.

So we did what we knew best and sat patiently because there was really nothing more we could do. It was up to the neighbors now. We never got upset, we adapted, knowing fully well that this too would pass. Unable to work inside the shuttered store, we made the sidewalk our meeting place. Slowly we started to become a fixture in the neighborhood. But the neighborhood kept tight vigilance over us; we never knew by whom or how, but we felt it.

While some focused on not letting us open, we focused on showing who we really were: a friendly family willing to work for the betterment of the neighborhood. Little by little, we began winning the neighbors' support. A few knew and loved us from our other locations that were not too far away but in a tougher part of town. These neighbors became are advocates. They were our voices and the leaders who stood up for us. They held all involved accountable, including us, to make sure things got done in a just manner. We were fielding hundreds of calls and mail kept pouring in. Unfortunately, the more we tried, the less we could do to help our own situation. We did everything by the book, but it was thrown out the window. It was humbling to see our neighbors taking on the fight on their own and us having to take a back seat. It seemed like our neighbors wanted the store opened even more than we anticipated. They energized us and gave us greater resolve to keep moving *pa'lante* - onward.

With little to be done, every day either Billy, John, Dad or I would spend countless hours just standing on the sidewalk of our closed location. Since we weren't allowed to even sweep the inside of the building, we began to sweep the sidewalks around the building and across the street. Making sure everything was tidy and presentable from the outside. We met so many people who stopped by for a gallon of milk only to find the store doors closed. We introduced ourselves, invited them to visit our other locations and made deliveries to their home. Soon we began taking orders right on the sidewalk, calling it into a nearby location just so that the community was served. We began having regular conversations, getting familiar with each other.

As the warmer months arrived, more and more people began to see us in our Foodtown shirts sweeping or having a meeting on the sidewalks. During those two and half years, we would hold our vendor and manager meetings on that sidewalk. We'd stand there and negotiate the price on a trailer of goods or pallets of soda. As time went on, neighbors would see our free home delivery van bringing in grocery orders just across the street from our closed shop and around town

Finally, we started a blog to keep the neighbors informed of every minute detail of the process with pictures and renderings of what the new location would look like. It was a place where they could comment and learn about everything that was happening or not. I do believe that the voices and support from our neighbors were instrumental in allowing us to finally open the store. I will be forever grateful to them and will make sure to always be of service to them. Eventually we opened to great success and are proud to have become a part of such a wonderful community.

Life Lesson

Be adaptable and learn to pivot when needed. Do not lose sight of your vision and your end goal. Sit patiently and observe. Be you - turn every negative into a positive. Be humble and allow those that can help lead the way. They may just be your biggest advocates.

18
Professionals

These are professionals working here. They may not be a professional in the sense of the word that we've been accustomed or trained to believe. Maybe they have not gone to university or maybe they have. Maybe they've gone to the School of Hard Knocks, but these are professionals who take great care in providing the service to our neighbors and making an honest wage. They're putting their children through college, paying mortgages, buying homes, and contributing positively to their community.

These are professionals but sometimes people would like to look down upon them. These are the same people who make up our neighborhoods and our communities and help to assist others. They have a conversation with the widow or the homebound person and maybe are their only connection to the outside world. These are the folks tending to the cases and the stocking of it all, but they also have the same dreams and desires that everyone has. Whether or not they have that fancy diploma from a college, it's our duty to help them reach and achieve those goals so that they can level up in their own lives.

We've had people who have told us we are the stability in their lives because there's so much drama that surrounds them at home they look forward to coming to work. Not only do we give them the opportunity to make a living, but we also show them how to become a better person and how to not accept the circumstances that may be in front of them. We show them that they can make a change for the better, to change those circumstances, to become someone else, to do something else, to do more for themselves and their families.

I get great satisfaction when someone who has been with us for years, (or even a short time) moves on, and gets a better position somewhere else. It lets them do something better for themselves, and they are able to use the training and the skills that they learned and earned with us. They come back and say, "Wow, you guys taught me a lot. It has really helped me at my new job. It's made a difference, and I recently got a promotion." Those things matter. Those things are important because they show that the person has grown from what many may see as a simple cashier job, for example, to something more. That "simple job" is much more than just that.

Life Lesson

It is not the title or degree on the wall that matters. What matters is how you do your job. Take pride in what you do and do your best. Respect those that you are working with. Know that you can make the difference in providing the best result.

19
The Food Desert Myth

In New York City and many other places in the USA, a common misconception that politicians and academics push forward is that of the Food Desert*. Food deserts are defined by the USDA as parts of the city/country lacking fresh fruit, vegetables, and other healthful whole foods. It usually refers to impoverished areas. This is largely due to a lack of grocery stores, farmers' markets, and healthy food providers. Many times politicians want to paint over in broad strokes the efforts of the independent store owners to provide fresh, healthy fruits, vegetables, quality meat and dairy, and the full service supermarkets, bodegas and fruit stores. Many of these are owned and operated by immigrants like Asians, Arabs, and Dominicans, all working side by side providing a service and filing a void left over from the bigger chains that operate in the city. As the bigger chains left the city to open up in the suburbs, their departure gave way to a new kind of operator who could serve and prosper in those same communities that the bigger chains did not want to serve.

The independents adapted well into the fabric of each neighborhood while catering to the specific ethnic groups, along with providing jobs to the local residents and investing in infrastructure - stores that the bigger companies did not want to invest in. These communities are continually being served with items from back home, be it Russian, Polish, Jamaican, Asian or Latin items, alongside the American brands. While there may be places where fresh food, fruits and vegetables might be difficult to find, I for one have always been able to find independent operators in any community. From Chicago to Florida and everywhere in between, independent operators will always fill the void and serve those that others will not. I now see the term "Food Desert" as more of a weapon. It's a way for local politicians and the bigger companies who are now looking to come back into the cities they abandoned during the suburban exodus, to get tax exemption deals, no interest loans, and expedited permits. These are often policies not offered to the independent operator. As independent operators, it is our duty to keep abreast of what is happening, see it, recognize it, adapt and begin to change as the business demands it. As neighborhoods change, we need to have a pulse on what's going on so that we are not caught blindsided. And while some of the neighborhoods become more gentrified, it gives us the opportunity to be the quirky store with unique offerings from back home.

*Food Desert term brought to forefront by Marion Nestle, Professor at NYU, author of Food Politics

Life Lesson

Learn to adapt quickly and get involved with your local community government. Know what and how the decisions being made will affect your business and be ready to make the necessary changes to remain profitable.

20
Business is Personal

We've had our fair share of growing pains ranging from theft by vendors or bad hires, to losing out on making the correct margins. We even had to overcome poor cash management. With so many pieces to oversee and manage, we knew we had to get better at hiring and training at our locations. Helping our team grow professionally and personally guaranteed a better work environment. It helped to create a team that is eager to help because they know we are there to help them. We have sought out consultants and coaches to improve on our systems and processes; helping us to grow in an ever changing landscape.

Sustainable growth didn't come without some struggles. The key was to overcome those struggles with better skills and techniques for our business and team. Seeking out the inefficiencies and getting comfortable with the uncomfortable came with taking on new challenges that enabled us to serve our neighbors better.

We knew that if we were able to improve the communities we serve, then our neighbors would in turn support us, allowing us to give greater opportunities to our team members and benefiting the business as a whole.

Many say that business is not personal but I would argue that it can only be personal. Knowing the names of your neighbors and understanding their wants and desires allows for a better relationship to grow between us and them. It makes for a better community. People are no longer wanting to just be done with the transaction, they want a place where they feel at home. A place like *Cheers* where everyone knows your name and exactly how you like your groceries bagged, your favorite kind of apple and the best steak to put on the grill.

Life Lesson

Show some care in your business and all you do. Adding a bit of care into things costs you nothing, but reaps you countless rewards. People enjoy doing business with those who add a personal touch. They will choose you over the guy that's just business and puts nothing into the relationship.

21
Good Samaritans

One of the greatest things I have been able to see is how many people Mami and Papi help. The great responsibility they have taken on. From being direct supporters of the local priest who has approximately 50 chapels and churches in all the surrounding neighborhoods, to feeding the poor, building houses, providing clothes, taking care of medical expenses and helping to send kids to school and college. They also helped push the federal government to renovate local schools and pave roads so people could travel easier.

After more than 30 years of trying to work with local, state, and federal politicians in the Dominican Republic, my father finally has realized a dream of his, and the extended communities of San Jose de Las Matas (Sajoma). He convinced the government to pave the dirt road connecting two major cities. Since he was a child, the road that connected Corozo and neighboring towns to Sajoma was a rutted, crater-filled dirt road without much access to the outside world. Dad had a vision that a new modern road would allow progress to trickle down from the bigger cities to the farmlands. It was a mission he largely took upon himself and never lost sight of by contributing his time, money, and resources. That determination of not giving up and wanting to serve his community was finally rewarded in 2015 when about 50 miles of asphalt was laid between the cities of Sajoma and Moncion. The humble dirt road was finally paved and now connected to the national highway system of the Dominican Republic.

But of all the people they helped, there's one particular story that moves me the most: it was 2013 and Dad was driving back home to Corozo as he passed a Haitian family of five walking in the sweltering heat. There were two men, two women with a young girl about 6 years old. One of the women was very far into her pregnancy. He zoomed past them but when he arrived home, it hit him. He couldn't let the Haitian family continue on without helping them. Jumping back in the car, he skidded out just as fast as he got home while yelling out the window to Mami, "Preparen algo de comer para una familia!" - prepare enough food for a family. Mom rushed into the kitchen and began to unload the contents of the fridge and pantry onto the kitchen table and counter. She had no idea who was coming to dinner, but understood by Dad's voice that they were important. Mom calls out to everyone within earshot at home to drop what they are doing and prepare for whoever it is that Dad is bringing home.

It didn't take long for Dad to catch back up to the slow trekkers. But took a bit longer to convince them that his intentions were righteous. Finally, they get in, and Dad races back home with the Haitian family in tow. Like many migrants, Haitians are looking for a better place to call home and are often searching for refuge inside the Dominican Republic. The journey to reach the Dominican Republic is a long hard road. Not everyone is kind towards them and that day they themselves took a risk by getting into Dad's car. Upon seeing Dad with his guests, Mom begins to bark out orders, "Get clean towels, prepare a room, start chopping onions, catch that chicken!" to everyone around. The guests that night would be a Haitian family of five that Mom and Dad demanded be taken care of just as well as when dignitaries or businessmen visited.

Mom washed all their clothes and hung them to dry. She also found gently used clothes for all to wear and keep. She invited them into our home with open arms, giving them comfortable beds to sleep in, a bathroom to wash in, shoes and all the food they could eat. Everyone ate together and learned about their journey, and became grateful to be in each other's company. While Mom and Dad encouraged them stay longer, they chose to take to the road again. But this time, they had more than a day's supply of food and drink to help them along. Unfortunately, I was not home that day but the story still moves me. I strive to have just a bit of the humility and compassion Mom and Dad show every day. To give as they do. To feel as they do. It's our responsibility to continue to contribute to those around us and never miss out on an opportunity to help someone else.

Another story that captures the commitment and dedication of our family, and the choices we face each day, happened across the street from one of our stores.

Not long ago there were two guys fighting on the street and a crowd was forming. No one wanted to get involved. Some looked on in shock while others watched in amusement. As one guy fell between two parked cars, John, who was at the store's entrance, saw what was happening. He yells at them to cut it out, and to every-one's surprise, they did and each walked away. While everyone else chose to just watch or rush past, John decided to say something. He made a choice for his neighbors and they thanked him. He said something because he cares. Later in the day, even one of the guys that had been fighting came into the store and apologized to John, telling him "Sorry, I just lost my cool and it won't happen again." It was as if he needed to explain himself to John. He, too, made a choice to stop fighting and recognized that there are people in the community that cared.

While these are just a couple of the examples, it's actions like these that motivate me to find even more ways for me and my family to make meaningful contributions to the communities we serve and live in. Sometimes it even keeps me up at night because I want to see that my children grow up to be givers and not takers. I'm proud to be an Estevez and grateful for all the blessings God gives us each day. We really have a lot to be thankful for. But at the same time, I cannot forget the responsibility I have to my family. I must teach them to always look to contribute more than they expect to get back.

Life Lesson

You must always be vigilant to the needs of others and be on the lookout for ways in which you can make a positive impact on some one's life. Do it without expecting anything back in return. Do it because you can and it is the right thing to do.

22
Opportunity and Obligation

I now see the advantages of growing up in a bicultural household where we were taught the customs and traditions of the Dominican Republic as well as American values. I find that I have a unique insight into two worlds which gives me a greater ability to understand and mold my own identity. It allows for a deeper understanding of others and helps to view things from different perspectives. There have been times when some people have seen me as not Dominican enough, and others see me as not American enough. Or poor enough or rich enough. Neither of those labels means much to me. I don't see a distinction between the two. What I always see for myself is being the best representative of me that I could be. I focus more on what I need to do in order to grow; things like reading and exposing myself to new worlds. Because my Dad was already taking us to tons of meetings with professional corporate types as we were growing up, I was able to talk to them about a wide range of topics. They were often surprised that I had read a lot of the most popular business books around-- sometimes even before they have had a chance to read them. In those meetings, I was able to show the Estevez family is not just about selling cans, and was more diverse and culturally literate than expected.

I also see the opportunities and obligations were offered to me. As a son of immigrant parents who ingrained in me a strong work ethic and faith, I take advantage of the opportunities presented to me while respecting the obligation that they require. My parents created an abundant amount of opportunities for me and my siblings which included a great education in business. They left their home country, as countless others have, seeking greater opportunities for themselves and their families. They did not know what they would find, but recognized the opportunity and advantage of fitting into the American way where one has the chance to be the best. So it is my obligation to keep moving forward and grabbing onto those opportunities that they have created. It would be irresponsible for me to do otherwise. More importantly, it would be disrespectful to their efforts and my own desires. It is my pleasure to take those opportunities and build upon them.

Now I want you too look closer at the word obligation. When you look at the root word of obligation, you get *oblige*, which means grateful or thankfulness. My obligation is more about the immense amount of gratitude I have for the opportunities laid before me. It is not a burden to endure. I ask you to reframe how you think about your own obligations and think of them as gifts to unwrap revealing opportunities to take and build upon.

It would be a great travesty for us to ignore or not appreciate the efforts and sacrifices others have given to allow us to live the life we are living. To me opportunity plus obligation equals growth. When you appreciate and respect the opportunities and obligations before you, you will be able to create a better world for those around you. It is my deep desire to keep creating more for my family and team so they too can create even greater opportunities for others.

Life Lesson

Remember that

Opportunity + Obligation = Growth

It is your job to make the best effort with the opportunities you are given, whether they come through your family or your boss. However, understand when taking on a new opportunity you have a commitment, an obligation, to those who are counting on you.

23
Learning to Listen by Speaking Up

Early on I learned to stand up for myself and speak up. Dad would push us, getting under our skin, whether intentionally or not, and we were forced to react. There were only a few choices—cry, tighten up, do and say nothing, or speak out. Each one was tried, abandoned, taken up again, and abandoned by the one trying to figure out what the heck he wanted or was saying. Finally, we each ended up figuring out that by using our voices, we could and would move the focus from us and toward something else. So we got better and better at finding the words to move the focus and get what we wanted—out of his spotlight. It was not wrath or tyranny. It was a psychological back-and-forth, and Dad loved playing mind games. And still does.

Mind you, speaking up to your father, in a typical Latin household, is unheard of and will not go unpunished. That wasn't the case at our house. We were expected to have conversations, give opinions, share observations, and debate - though some would call it arguing. We were loud, talking over one another. Dad would just listen. We didn't know it then, but we were to listen and interpret and know how to read between the lines. We learned how to convince, persuade, and soothe. Dad taught us that no two situations were the same, so you needed to figure each out. With some people you cater to their egos while others their humility. But it must always be done with respect so that you are able to get what you want. It won't always work, but sometimes it is helpful altering yourself a bit and mimicking the other person's way of speaking, be it slang, pop culture, or current events, and having the ability to change back and forth between English and Spanish, or Spanglish. It is important to know how to adapt on the fly from conversing with the old Jewish grandmother or the dude from the corner. Our ability and willingness to treat them with equal respect and make them feel welcomed enabled us to learn how to do business in so many different types of neighborhoods and to change along with them as time has gone by.

Today I am proud to say that we operate stores in neighborhoods ranging from yuppie to upwardly mobile urban ones, and mixed ethnic lower-income ones. We strive to provide the right mix to the communities we serve with the freshest fruits and vegetables to high-quality meat products. We offer particular cuts of meat and vegetables that the neighbors could only find in their home country, and play the music they grew up with within our stores. We become part of each neighborhood and seek team members with the same welcoming mentality. We want our neighbors to feel welcomed and to look at us as part of their extended family.

I've received countless letters thanking us for bringing in "that seasoning my mama used back at home." I've been stopped by our neighbors so many times in the aisle, telling me how wonderful or helpful one of our team members has been to his grandmother or daughter. We are lucky to be in communities where the people living there take pride in what they have and strive to keep a healthy and uplifting environment for their families.

One of the best gifts we've enjoyed is when one of our neighbors comes up directly to Dad or one of us and lets us know if they have had a bad experience in one of our stores. They do this because they know and see us working and striving every day, just as they themselves are doing. By sharing a negative experience, they know they are giving us important information that we'll use to make improvements. They know that saying something makes a difference and they trust us to make it right and not allow it to happen again. Our neighbors take ownership for their store, helping us improve in ways that only they are able to express.

Life Lesson

No matter to whom you are talking, be sure to always treat them with the same respect you want to be treated with.

24
No Comparison

Even as children, Dad and Mom would speak to us as if we were adults, clearly and without the pretensions that a child could not understand. Treating us with the same respect they expected of us for them and everyone else. They loved us immensely but didn't coddle us. When we saw friends do this, we were reminded that in the Estevez family we do things a little differently than everyone else. So we learned to never compare ourselves or keep count of what another has or doesn't.

Mom and Dad told us to be proud of ourselves and when we found ourselves drifting, to say a small prayer because God keeps blessing that person and helps you to reach your own goals. They warned of times when people would gossip (and they were right) and try to speak ill of us or someone else. They taught us to learn to listen, but not "hear" the gossip and never repeat it. If we did, we would have to deal with the consequences of being "*en la boca de otro*" - on the lips of others. Gossip never did or will help you in anyway. Many times someone would try to whisper into my ears a lie about someone close to me, trying to create a rift between my brothers or sister, and thankfully we never were swayed by the falsehoods. Instead, we'd address and stop it right there immediately and without any hesitation. We'd then might discuss it privately with each other if need be. Mark Twain said it best, "comparison is the death of joy." Rather than comparing oneself to others, be happy for them and get onto what is most important to you.

They also trusted us to make the right choices, like when they allowed John, Maggie, and me to ride the bus to bible study classes alone on Sunday from New Jersey to Washington Heights. Not too many kids did this on their own, but again we were being taught about trust and responsibility by doing, rather than by being given a lecture. After our bus ride, we would meet up with cousins then head to church with aunts and uncles, spending the rest of the day in New York at our aunt and uncles, Lucila and Pachango, apartment on 175th street. Being the youngest, I was forced to stay inside with the girls and watched from the fire escape as John and my cousins Dennis, Gabriel and other kids on the block would play stick ball, skeelys (a game kind of like marbles but with bottle caps) and cool off in the open fire hydrant. When it got too hot to bear in the apartment, I begged my aunt to let me go down and play in the fire hydrant with the older boys. The fun of running in an open hydrant, even for a few minutes, was and still is a lot of fun for New York City kids. Whenever the fire department truck came by to shut off the water, it was always turned back on by the time they turned the corner. John, Maggie and I made sure to be on our best behavior on those visits because we definitely didn't want to lose out on visiting our cousins.

Life Lesson

Do not keep a tally of what someone else has. Comparing yourself to someone else will only bring on feeling of envy. Be happy for the success of others. Enjoy and celebrate your own successes and keep on improving up them.

25
Neighbors Serving Neighbors

It used to be that to buy a gallon of milk, eggs, and bread you needed to stop at a supermarket or maybe a bodega. Not anymore. Almost everywhere you go today, you can buy grocery items. If you're having dinner at a restaurant, you can buy their secret sauce or drink mix, add it to your bill, and enjoy it at home. As you go about your day, notice how many places sell what used to be traditional grocery items only sold at a supermarket. There's hair salons selling drinks and snacks next to their shampoo and conditioner. At the coffee shop you can pick up a pound of your favorite coffee beans. Gas stations have become mini-marts with cellophane-wrapped produce and jerky in every size and flavor. And probably the most common is the local pharmacies selling everything from Lipitor to beer, peanut butter, and frozen pizzas.

Never has it been easier for someone to replenish a dozen eggs. It's almost like no one ever needs to step into a supermarket again.

However, what is the big missing piece for the shopper getting their groceries from any one of these places? If you said freshness of product—fresh produce, fresh baked goods, fresh meat—as well as variety, high quality, and competitive prices—you would be correct.

But I believe the most important factor is *our* team members. Each and every one of them brings a unique quality to the team. We are lucky to have them. The team makes all the difference because a can of corn is a can of corn anywhere you go. But making a connection with Al behind the delicatessen counter cannot be manufactured. Not everywhere has got a team that genuinely cares for the products they are selling and your enjoyment of them. Providing every neighbor who steps through our door a friendly and welcoming place to visit and shop at is what we strive for at Estevez Foodtown. And we are blessed to have the caring team that we do. Too many people expect poor customer service that they are easily satisfied just by being able to get in and out of the store as quickly as possible. Showing a bit of care in everything you do goes a long way.

A great customer experience begins even before your neighbor steps into the store. From the moment they are writing up their list and thinking about what to cook for dinner and how they will serve it to their family, in the back of their minds they're thinking of the store where they can get the freshest cut of USDA choice beef and farm fresh produce along with all the family favorites. I want them to think of Estevez Foodtown as an extension of their pantry.

Our team members are the ones who makes the difference for our neighbors to choose us rather than stopping at a competitor on the way home. A simple "Hello" or "Good morning," as you pass each other in the aisles, asking if they need help finding something and taking them directly to the shelf. Doing this shows you care. And putting a bit of caring in everything you do doesn't cost anything and brightens every-one's day.

One of the great things I love to see is when a new mother comes in to show off her new baby girl to all the cashiers and the rest of the team because they genuinely care, and later the team asks about both mom and baby to the father on one of his diaper runs

Our shoppers are our neighbors. We live, work, and strive together. So when you greet them by name, "Hola, Senora Garcia," - Hello Mrs. Garcia - you're welcoming her into the Estevez Foodtown family and building a positive relationship with you. In a sense, you really are making her feel right at home within the aisles.

But customer service goes beyond saying hello. It is teaching your neighbor's daughter, on her run to the store for mom, the difference between parsley and cilantro. It is supporting the Little League and Girl Scouts, helping stock the food bank at the local church. Customer service is really about following the Golden Rule, treating your neighbor just as you wish to be treated.

When we begin to see people not just as another customer but as our neighbor, we really open ourselves up to building a relationship with them. Good neighbors help each other. They stop and chat and wish you a good day. A great neighbor watches out for you and becomes an extended member of your family. A great neighbor cares just as much about you and your family as he does his/her own.

I strive each day to be that great neighbor to all the people we serve from our shoppers, teams, and vendors. Because with one looking out for the other, we will improve our communities together.

It is why I want to redefine how we look and treat our customers. First of all, let's stop calling them customers or even shoppers. At Estevez Foodtown our customers are our neighbors, so we will treat them as such. Let's see past the customer transaction and count and measure our success by how well we treat and get along with our neighbors. Be the kind of place where moms chat in the aisles and teachers catch up with past students. Where a dad heads over to talk about last night's game with the produce manager behind a mountain of bananas.

The basic definition of a good neighbor is someone who is friendly and cooperative and works to the betterment of their community. They support each other in good and bad times. A good neighbor is interested in how well you are doing. Not just walking past you, acting as if they never even saw you.

Through service we strive to be an integral part of the communities we serve.

To serve is to be of use with trust and respect while helping others. For us it is not a job, and we do not want people to just show up to work because they see it as just another j-o-b, or see our neighbors as a disturbance and something to get past. We want team members to treat our neighbors as guests — helping the mom of 3 unload her cart onto the counter and helping the grandmother grab a jar of artichokes that's out of reach.

When we choose to view all who come through our doors as our neighbors, we open ourselves up to making new friends, to opportunity, and to growing the business.

We need to look at coming to work as a privilege to serve our neighbors. Becoming interested in their lives and they will be in yours. One of my greatest pleasures is when a neighbor brings in a small plate of food from the BBQ they're having to one of our team members. Or seeing a cashier's tears well up when neighbor after neighbor asks her about how well her new baby is doing, offering the new mom advice and sometimes giving her a gift of an outfit and booties for her new baby. Or the woman who loves to bake that brings in cookies and cakes for the entire team. Keep in mind these are ingredients she bought in our store, went home, prepped, baked, and brought back to us. That shows care and appreciation.

For years and still until this day, my brother's John and Billy, receive cakes or cookies on their birthdays from our neighbors. Throughout the day you will hear neighbors singing Happy Birthday in the aisles and at the checkout lanes.

These seemingly small acts of kindness from our neighbors to our team are really a big show of gratitude. It's their way of saying, "Thank you," for providing such exceptional customer service and making an effort to know them. When you take an interest in some one's well-being, they can sense it and know it's genuine. Having a neighbor bring in a plate of warm home-baked cookies to you or someone on our team proves that you are, and by extension Estevez Foodtown, a big part of the community.

Some easy things you can do are: smile and greet them by name. Buy Girl Scout cookies. Allow them to try a product they have never tasted before they buy it. Ask about their son's little league team. Support their church, charity, or school play. Buy an ad in their journal. Walk them to their car. Say,

"Thank you." Send them something home to taste and try, no strings attached. Talk about last night's game. Compliment them on a new hairstyle. Congratulate them on a graduation or a new baby. The important thing is to be yourself. Get interested in them, and they will be interested in you.

Remember—our duty is to serve our neighbors well.

Life Lesson

Make meaningful connections with your neighbors, the people you work with, and begin to build a sense of community with them. Have fun at it. People enjoy being around those who make them feel comfortable and always have a smile on their face. Don't forget to show your appreciation.

Part Four:
Lessons for the Future

Leaving a Better Place

What do you have to release from your grasp now?

In order to make room for what is to come

Moving you past your past

Stepping up into a future that's bigger

You figured out

How the work of the present

Presents you with presents

To hand off to those who are present

Knowing that the powers within you

To create, mold, and disrupt

Getting your hands dirty

You're battle scarred

Standing tall

Stepping firm

All the while like Gandhi

Becoming the change you want to see in the world

26
The Relay Race

At the end of the day I see myself as a servant-leader, a term coined by Robert K. Greenleaf, who is recognized as a premier figure in leadership, education, management and religion. Greenleaf defines a servant-leader as someone who focuses primarily on the growth and well-being of people and the communities to which they belong. He or she is someone who is trusted and doesn't care about fancy titles. There are three primary groups that I proudly serve: my family, my team, and my neighbors - all of which make up *my family*. I hope to instill that same desire in each and expect nothing back in return except that they live a good, healthy life and become the best versions of themselves.

I will admit that I struggle at times with knowing if I'm making the right choices for my team and family so that they can live their best life. It is something that I spend a lot of time thinking about. I even found this entry in an old journal of mine talking about this topic:

January 16, 2012

Struggles

I struggle with finding a way to teach my kids, family, and team to live to their full potential.

I hope that they will be humble, honest, down-to-earth and have a fire to live to see the world through their own eyes.

I hope for them not to be consumers but creators.

Givers and not takers.

To add value to the community.

I struggle to be a father (leader) that expects the best and not force my own ideology onto them.

I struggle to be patient when tears roll down their cheeks because crying has never solved anything, even though I'll cry with the sappy commercial or movie.

I struggle with finding a way to teach them to use their minds to build and create and nurture and love and be a family together wherever their own path leads them.

How do I instill our values, beliefs and traditions for when we are gone they still have us?

A friend of mine, Lee Brower, once shared with me that life was more like a continuous relay race, which has helped in easing my own mental struggle. He explains it not a sprint or even a marathon, but a relay race that continues as each generation passes the baton to the next generation. Collecting and gathering all the family's wisdom and preparing the next generation to be able to run the next leg. But the thing about races is that no one finishes at the same time. Everyone has a different pace. No matter, we all need to be well enough to take the baton when it's passed onto us.

You cannot be eating donuts on the sidelines and expecting a trophy at the finish line.

It is our duty to make sure that all the family and team members have their sneakers laced up, are properly warmed up, know their start times, and are ready to take the baton. They are ready to face the challenges up ahead. They are able to recover quickly and efficiently when a baton gets dropped.

I am running the extra mile for my family, with my family.

The goal is to enjoy our leg of the race - the journey. I fully expect that when the baton gets passed onto me, I will have a firm grip to be able to carry it onto the next generation. I'm grateful knowing that I'll be running alongside my wife, Ingrid and siblings John, Maggie, and Billy and all those great souls that are part the Estevez team.

Life Lesson

Capture today what you want the next generation to know. Teach, guide, and nurture them. Allow them to fall and be ready to pick them up. Share and show them from where you've come and where you want to go. Empower them so that they will be ready to lead when it is their turn.

Epilogue

Simply put, the unfair advantage I believe that we have had as a family has been the unity and the respect we hold for one another from the oldest to the youngest. This combined with a strong work ethic and the ability to separate business, personal, and family issues. Even though we work together and may have a disagreement at work (or home), five minutes later we are friends. We are all accountable, all the time, to the business and to the family. Within the business, each respects his or her role and responsibilities. They are always expected to do their best. Outside of the business, we also spend a lot of time together. I can proudly say that we are not only family, we are the best of friends. Of course there are challenges, but we always look to rectify any issues that arise immediately. It helps that we are all working towards a common goal and shared mutual vision.

Our perseverance has been a direct result of our parent's attitude, who never let any obstacles get in their way. There is nothing that helps to create stronger bonds with others than having struggled and succeeded alongside them. It's been a part of who we are and how every day each of us puts in the work and effort to improve the business, our team and ourselves.

In order to maintain the hunger in my belly, there are some fundamental questions that I carry within me:

How do we become the best versions of ourselves?

How do we help the next generation get there too?

How do we as the leaders of our team serve them better and guide them to reach their full potential inside and outside the business?

How do we make our communities better?

Finally, how do we make sure that an entitlement mentality does not set into our team, our children and ourselves?

These are hard questions to answer. I do not have the answers, but I promise I will work to find them because the success of those that I serve. My family, team, and community is my "why" for getting up energized every morning.

Nevertheless, if we choose to call ourselves leaders, there is a choice we need to make, every day. Individually and collectively we must ask how can we best contribute? This is especially important as the team and family grow and the business expands. Making the right choices and pooling all of our individual talents together will help push us to the next level. Imagine what we will be able to accomplish when the collective energy of the new generation joins with us to elevate each other, the team, family, and our communities.

The challenge will be for us not to wait for outside circumstances to force us to act under pressure, but to begin leveraging our strengths to become the best versions of ourselves. While never forgetting what my father has always asked of us, "Que vas a contribuir?" What will you contribute? While continuing to be faithful servants who take bold action for the betterment of our family, team and community.

Acknowledgements

First off I want to thank God for the many blessings he has given me.

To the love of my life, Ingrid, whose continued support, dedication, and patience I could not do without - thank you for all you do for us.

To Isabella, Amber, and Matthew because of you I am.

Bendiciones, Mami y Papi, gracias por su gran ejemplo y ser los mejores padres del mundo para mi y mis hermanos.

John – what can I say – Thank you for your vision. Billy, you are the leader I wish to become. Maggie - thank you for being who you are and always keeping us in your prayers.

Lucila y Pachango, bendiciones!

To Francia, Jonas, Priscilla, Magdaline, Emmanuel, Hilda, Gabriel, Yisell, Kendal, Ava, GP, Dennis, Ramon, Jose, Manny, Maritza, Millie, Maria, Lauren, Nellie, Melissa, and my entire Estevez, Rodriguez, Gomez, Checo, and extended families. Gracias Negra, Neris, Anny, Angela, Rolando, Juan, Belkis, Fausto, Jose Luis, Ambiorix, and Jhon. Plus all 125 cousins, nieces and nephews thank you for your commitment and dedication in keeping us a united, fun-loving, hard-working, and loud family.

To Arron, Sam, Joe, and Tomas thank you making us better.

Let me not forget the great organizations and groups for their support the Allegiance staff and Foodtown co-op, Krasdale Foods and our vendor community, National Supermarket Association, Friday Group, altMBA, SPS, Breakthrough Blueprint, Strategic Coach, and Wacky Warriors.

Finally, to all the great communities we serve and to our amazing team gracias por todo.

Made in the USA
Middletown, DE
05 February 2019